# Cambridge Elements

Elements in the Economics of Emerging Markets
edited by
Bruno S. Sergi
*Harvard University*



# FROM COLLECTIVE PUNISHMENT TO CONSTRAINTS ON AUTHORITY

## *Rethinking the Impact of US Sanctions on Venezuela*

Miguel Angel Santos
*Tecnologico de Monterrey, School of Government and Public Transformation*

José Morales-Arilla
*Tecnologico de Monterrey, School of Government and Public Transformation*

Zinedine Partipilo Cornielles
*Harvard University*

CAMBRIDGE
UNIVERSITY PRESS

CAMBRIDGE
UNIVERSITY PRESS

Shaftesbury Road, Cambridge CB2 8EA, United Kingdom

One Liberty Plaza, 20th Floor, New York, NY 10006, USA

477 Williamstown Road, Port Melbourne, VIC 3207, Australia

314–321, 3rd Floor, Plot 3, Splendor Forum, Jasola District Centre, New Delhi – 110025, India

Cambridge University Press is part of Cambridge University Press & Assessment, a department of the University of Cambridge.

We share the University's mission to contribute to society through the pursuit of education, learning and research at the highest international levels of excellence.

www.cambridge.org
Information on this title: www.cambridge.org/9781009704304

DOI: 10.1017/9781009704274



First published 2026

*A catalogue record for this publication is available from the British Library*

*A Cataloging-in-Publication data record for this Element is available from the Library of Congress*

ISBN 978-1-009-70430-4 Hardback
ISBN 978-1-009-70428-1 Paperback
ISSN 2631-8598 (online)
ISSN 2631-858X (print)

# From Collective Punishment to Constraints on Authority

## Rethinking the Impact of US Sanctions on Venezuela

Elements in the Economics of Emerging Markets

DOI: 10.1017/9781009704274
First published online: April 2026

---

Miguel Angel Santos
*Tecnologico de Monterrey, School of Government and Public Transformation*

José Morales-Arilla
*Tecnologico de Monterrey, School of Government and Public Transformation*

Zinedine Partipilo Cornielles
*Harvard University*

**Author for correspondence:** Miguel Angel Santos, miguelsantos@tec.mx

**Abstract:** This Element critically examines the claim that United States economic sanctions on Venezuela constituted "collective punishment" of the Venezuelan population, contributing significantly to the country's economic collapse and humanitarian crisis. Through comprehensive analysis of economic, developmental, and welfare indicators from 2013 to 2023, it demonstrates that the bulk of Venezuela's economic devastation – including 52 percent of GDP losses and 98 percent of import declines – largely occurred before financial sanctions were imposed in August 2017. Key welfare indicators such as infant mortality, undernourishment, and life expectancy had deteriorated substantially by 2017 and subsequently stabilized or improved following sanctions implementation, contradicting narratives that attribute Venezuela's collapse primarily to external economic pressure. The Element provides a timeline of Venezuelan economic and political events around sanctions and a critical review of the literature on their economic effects. This title is also available as Open Access on Cambridge Core.

**Keywords:** economic sanctions, Venezuela, political economy, development, causal inference, authoritarian governance, sanction-proofing



ISBNs: 9781009704304 (HB), 9781009704281 (PB), 9781009704274 (OC)
ISSNs: 2631-8598 (online), 2631-858X (print)

# Contents

# 1 Introduction

The use of economic sanctions has become increasingly common as a tool of foreign policy. While the motives behind the enactment of sanctions are often political, a substantive portion of debates regarding sanctions has to do with their economic consequences and developmental side effects on the population. Estimates about their effectiveness are hotly contested (Pape, 1997; Elliott, 1998; Pape, 1998; Hufbauer et al., 2007), with recent estimates pointing to a 35% success or partial success rate between 2000 and 2016, with variation depending on the stated political objectives (Felbermayr et al., 2021).[1] Similarly contested is the literature regarding the economic effects on sanctioned countries: While there are studies favoring the view that sanctions induce a reduction in GDP growth rates and development outcomes (Neuenkirch and Neumeier, 2015, 2016, 2023), the endogenous nature of sanctions has been highlighted as a potential limitation to the validity of estimates in this literature (Kaempfer and Lowenberg, 2007; Kwon et al., 2020; Gutmann et al., 2020; Felbermayr et al., 2021).

Debates about cross-country average effects of sanctions are mirrored when discussing specific case studies. In this Element, we focus on the case of Venezuela, which was subject to financial sanctions and to oil sanctions from the United States in late 2017 and early 2019, respectively. On the one hand, sanctions have failed to deliver regime change and democratization, which was their stated objective. On the other hand, negotiations among the Maduro regime, the Venezuelan opposition, and the United States led to an election with a modicum of electoral conditions, in which the opposition was able to prove massive electoral fraud (Corrales and Kronick, 2025). Throughout these negotiations, the regime repeatedly demanded relief from economic sanctions as conditions for electoral concessions (Anadolu Agency, 2021; Itriago Acosta, 2022; Buitrago et al., 2023a, 2023b), suggesting that they were an effective negotiation tool. Whether these moderate and short concessions from the regime were worth it depends on a subjective assessment against the potential economic side effects that sanctions may have imposed on Venezuelans.

On this latter front, there is a sizable literature led by development economists arguing that sanctions worked as a "collective punishment" on Venezuelans. Jeffrey Sachs argued that the 2017 financial sanctions led to the death of 40,000 Venezuelans (Sachs and Weisbrot, 2019). Francisco Rodríguez recently asserted that sanctions led to more than half of Venezuela's economic

[1] According to Felbermayr et al. (2021), sanctions having democratization as a stated objective had a success/partial success rate above 80% between 2000 and 2016.

contraction and corresponding refugee crisis (Rodríguez, 2025a). The main purpose of this Element is to assess the merits of these claims. Our central finding is that the evidence does not support the "collective punishment" narrative. Using newly assembled datasets and a range of rigorous empirical methods, we show that the bulk of Venezuela's economic contraction and deterioration in welfare indicators took place prior to the imposition of sanctions, with no indication of incremental harm attributable to them thereafter.

To ground this assessment, we begin with a broad view of Venezuela's economic and developmental outcomes between 2013 and 2023.

In the following figures, we show the broad evolution of economic and developmental indicators for Venezuela around economic sanctions. In all these figures, the vertical dashed lines mark the August 2017 sanctions, these sanctions had a relatively limited scope, which we will refer to as "financial" sanctions and the January 2019 sanctions, which were much more stringent and we refer to as "oil" sanctions. The horizontal dotted lines mark the 2017 values of the variable being considered, which helps assess the share of the variation that occurred before economic sanctions.

Panel A of Figure 1 shows the evolution of Venezuela's yearly gross domestic product between 2013 and 2023. By 2017, real GDP had fallen by 37%, which represented 52% of the GDP loss between 2013 and 2023. We observe no acceleration in rate of collapse then, but a continuation of pre-sanctions trends - that is, had the Venezuelan economy continued to evolve as it was before sanctions were first enacted, we would observe very similar outcomes by 2020. Interestingly, the Venezuelan economic collapse comes to a halt in 2020–2021, right after the enactment of oil sanctions in 2019, and despite the COVID-19 pandemic.

Imports are a key link in the causal logic behind the argument that sanctions were a collective punishment on Venezuelans: By reducing Venezuela's oil exports, sanctions constrained the capacity for the country to sustain essential imports, in turn leading to the collapse of the economy, the death of thousands, and the migration of millions. Panel B of Figure 1 focuses on Venezuelan imports between 2013 and 2023. By 2017, imports had fallen by 77% when compared to 2013, constituting 98.5% of the import losses between 2013 and 2023. Notably, the rate of collapse in Venezuelan imports starts to attenuate in 2017, and imports start to grow in 2020, right after the 2019 sanctions and despite the COVID-19 pandemic.

Beyond economic outcomes, the argument of sanctions as a collective punishment on Venezuelans focuses on how they led to the massive collapse of Venezuelans' living standards. We now focus on fundamental health and

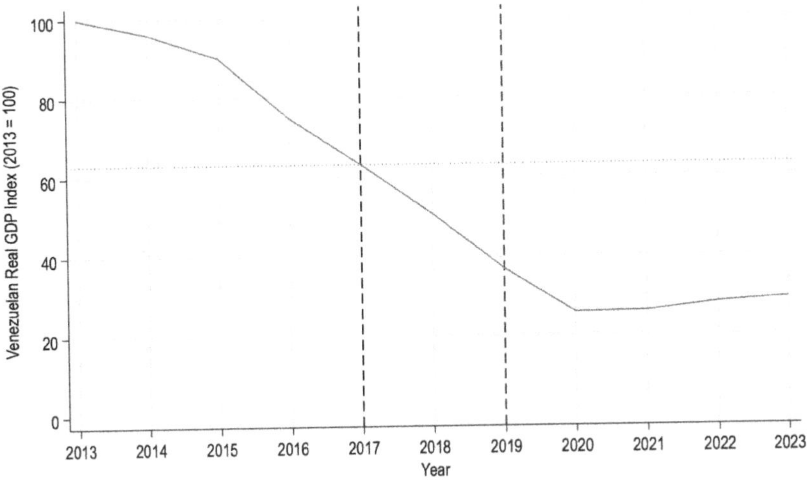


(a) Real GDP Index

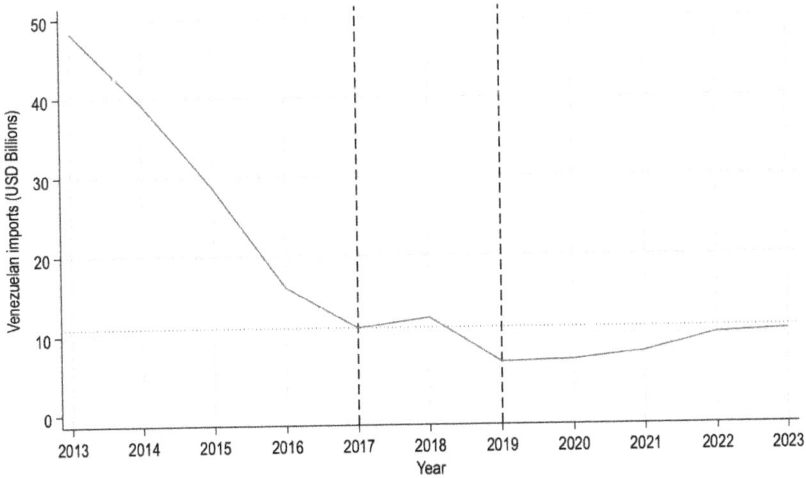


(b) Imports

**Figure 1** Venezuelan real GDP index and total imports, 2013–2023

**Note:** Panel A shows Venezuela's real GDP index (2013 = 100) from 2013 to 2023. Panel B shows total imports in billions of USD over the same period. Vertical dashed lines indicate the imposition of US financial sanctions (August 2017) and oil sanctions (January 2019). Horizontal dotted lines mark 2017 values.

**Sources:** IMF World Economic Outlook Database for real GDP; Harvard Growth Lab's Atlas of Economic Complexity for import data. Authors' calculations.

nutrition indicators capturing the evolution of such standards.[2] Panel A of Figure 2 shows the evolution of infant mortality rates as published by the World Bank's World Development Indicators (WDI) and the Economist Intelligence Unit (EIU). Infant mortality rates grew 40%–70% between 2013 and 2017, depending on the source. Fundamentally, both sources suggest that infant mortality rates stabilized in 2017–2018, and the EIU reference suggests they started to decrease between 2020 and 2021, after the 2019 sanctions and despite the COVID-19 pandemic. Panel B focuses on undernourishment rates as published by the WDI. This is a key variable to consider in the context of the collective-punishment logic, as it should be driven by worsening access to food imports. Undernourishment rates grew from 2.5% to 23.5% of the population -a more than eightfold increase- between 2013 and 2017, remaining stable after sanctions during 2018–2019, and starting to decrease between 2020 and 2022.

We now turn to indicators that reflect the capacity of sustaining life in Venezuela. Panel A of Figure 3 shows the evolution of Venezuelans' life expectancy at birth between 2013 and 2023, which dropped by 1.25 years between 2013 and 2017 and improved after financial sanctions, between 2017 and 2019. Life expectancy started to drop again between 2020 and 2021, as expected by the onset of the COVID-19 pandemic, but as the emergency ended, it quickly recovered to near-2015 levels. Panel B shows the country's crude death rates between 2013 and 2023, which grew by 18% between 2013 and 2017, and stabilized between 2017 and 2019. Again, as in previous indicators, crude death rates started to increase in 2020, stabilizing in 2022 once the COVID-19 pandemic ended.

Taken together, this broad view of Venezuelan economic and development indicators suggests that, with the exception of variables directly affected by the COVID-19 pandemic, the downward spiral of living standards that the country was experiencing before sanctions stabilized and started to improve in the aftermath of sanctions. It is true that we cannot observe what would have happened to these same outcomes had sanctions not been enacted, and the point could be made that they might have improved even further. But the argument that the country's demise was "deliberately caused by the United States, by what

[2] We focus on these development outcomes because of data availability issues in the post-sanctions period. In education terms, data from the WDI shows gross primary education enrollment rates drop by more than 6 percentage points between 2013 and 2017. Interestingly, enrollment rates improve by 1.4 percentage points by 2018. The WDI does not provide data for the years 2019–2022. However, it provides a datapoint for 2023 showing a complete recovery in enrollment rates in comparison to 2013 levels. For anecdotal evidence about worsening educational enrollment before financial sanctions were first enacted, see Lamas (2017).

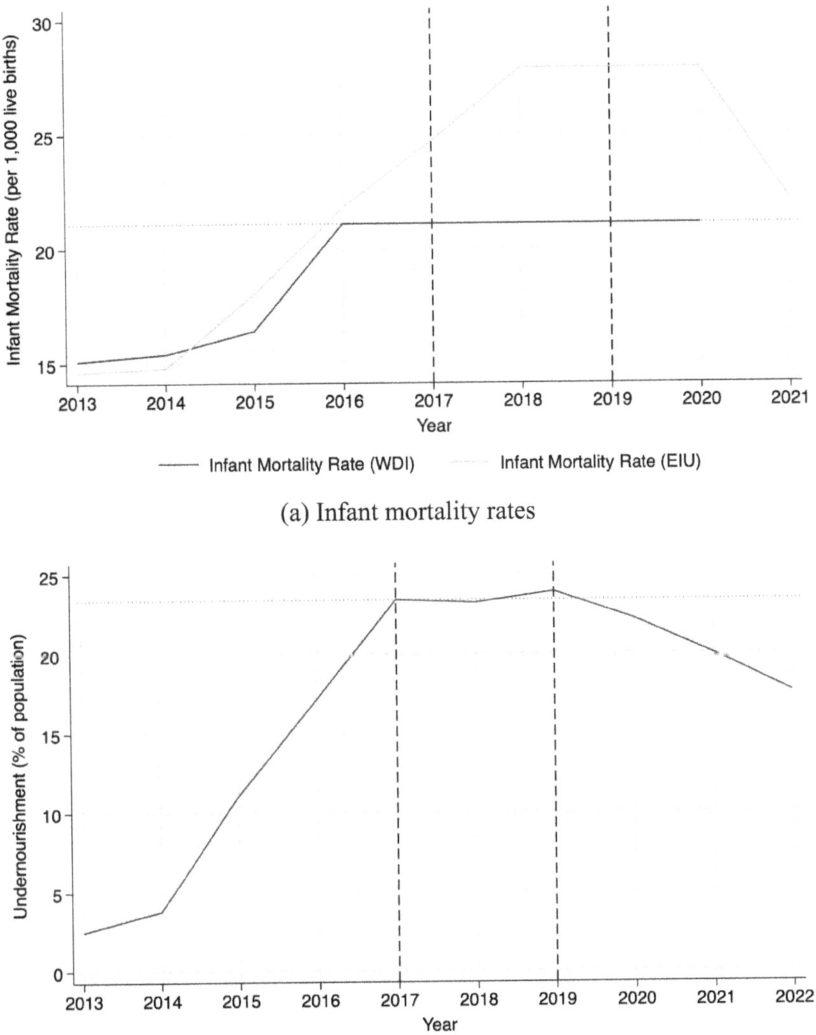


(a) Infant mortality rates

(b) Undernourishment rate

**Figure 2** Venezuelan infant mortality and undernourishment rates, 2013–2022

**Note:** Panel A shows infant mortality rates (deaths per 1,000 live births) from 2013 to 2021, with two data series from different sources. Panel B shows the prevalence of undernourishment as a percentage of the total population from 2013 to 2022. Vertical dashed lines indicate the imposition of US financial sanctions (August 2017) and oil sanctions (January 2019). Horizontal dotted lines mark 2017 values.

**Sources:** World Bank's World Development Indicators (WDI) and Economist Intelligence Unit (EIU) for infant mortality rates; WDI for undernourishment rates. Authors' calculations.

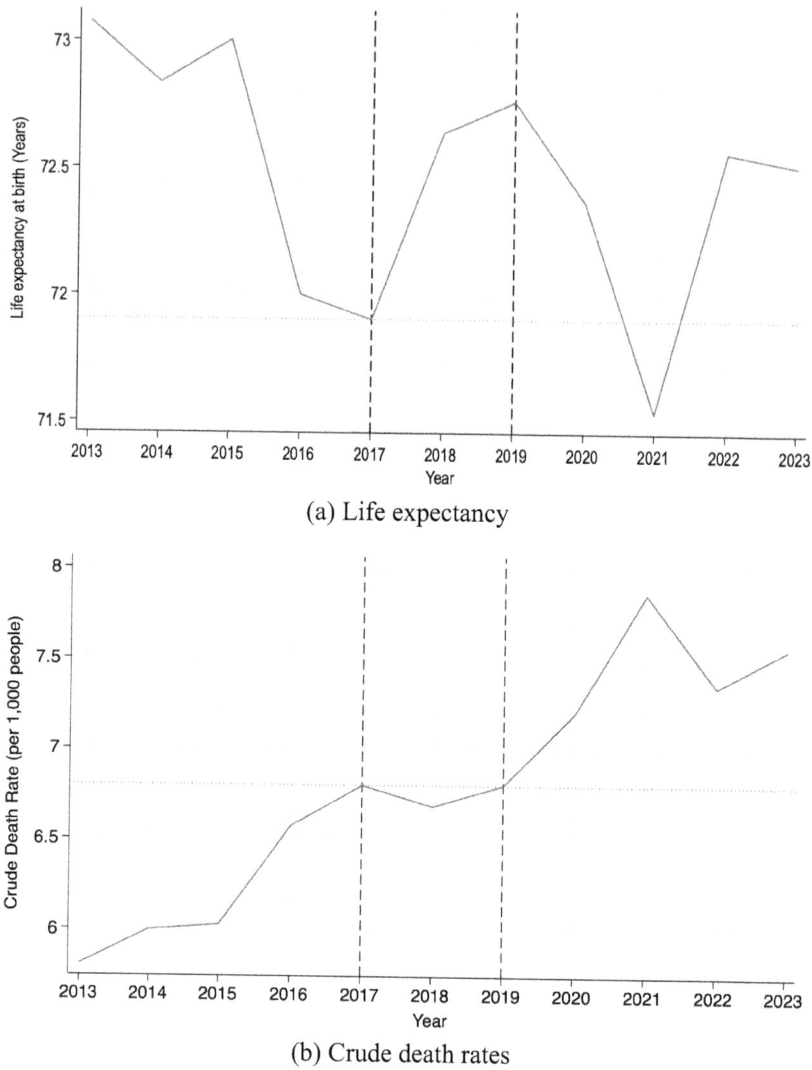


**Figure 3** Venezuelan life expectancy and crude death rates, 2013–2023

**Note:** Panel A shows life expectancy at birth in years from 2013 to 2023. Panel B shows crude death rates (deaths per 1,000 population) over the same period. Vertical dashed lines indicate the imposition of US financial sanctions (August 2017) and oil sanctions (January 2019). Horizontal dotted lines mark 2017 values.

**Sources:** World Bank's World Development Indicators (WDI). Authors' calculations.

I [J. Sachs] would say are illegal sanctions" (Democracy Now!, 2019) is inconsistent with the data. If the lion's share of economic and developmental collapses had occurred by the time sanctions were enacted, and if their worsening trends attenuated and started improving after sanctions, then it is extremely hard to justify statements that impute "52% of the Venezuelan economic collapse" and four out of the eight million Venezuelan refugees as a consequence of sanctions (Ruiz, 2025).

The next step is to move beyond this descriptive overview and evaluate the causal claims about the effects of sanctions on Venezuela.

If such statements are in opposition to this broadest view of the Venezuelan data, then what is the analytic substance behind them? In this Element, we first present a thorough timeline of political and economic events in Venezuela around sanctions, between 2013 and 2025. Building on this background, we then engage on a critical review of the quantitative causal literature about the effects of the financial and oil sanctions on the Venezuelan economy, considering contributions both in favor and against the view that they worked as a collective punishment on Venezuelans. Our conclusion is that the literature favoring that view does not overcome three fundamental concerns: 1)It does not engage with key intermediary economic indicators and developmental outcomes behind the "causal chain" logic of the argument; 2)it does not differentiate effects of sanctions from the continuation of pre-sanctions trends; and 3)it does not properly identify effects of either the 2017 financial or the 2019 oil sanctions from the effects of several concurrent treatments.

In response to this literature, this Element provides three pieces of novel independent analyses to overcome these concerns. First, we evaluate whether economic and migration patterns in oil-producing regions worsened disproportionately after sanctions were first enacted. We find that they did not. We then look at daily and field-specific oil production data on the days before and after the 2019 blackouts, which occurred about a month after the oil sanctions were enacted. We find massive negative effects of the blackouts, highlighting how concluding that worsening oil production after sanctions is a consequence of sanctions relies on confounding the effects of concurrent treatments and methodologically problematic identification strategies. Finally, we pursue a synthetic control methodology to evaluate whether Venezuelan essential imports dropped disproportionately after the enactment of sanctions. Once again, we find that they did not.

We then narrow our focus to Venezuela's foreign exchange controls and their decoupling around the enactment of sanctions. After describing their structure and profoundly negative effects on the country's economy and institutionality, we outline the different post-sanctions steps taken by the Maduro regime to progressively remove exchange controls. We then measure and describe overpricing in Venezuelan imports, one of the key corrosive consequences of exchange controls. We document that overpricing starts after exchange controls were first enacted in 2003, grows greatly with the start of the economic crisis, and peaks, in 2016. Then, they start to dwindle after 2017, and completely disappear after the 2019 oil sanctions.

It may be that exchange and price controls would have been removed in the absence of sanctions.[3] In that case, the stabilization and mild recovery that followed should not be considered a consequence of sanctions. However, analysts have argued and there is substantive anecdotal evidence indicating that such economic reforms were part of the regime's response to the increased economic pressure brought about by sanctions. If this was the case, then not only would have sanctions not induced the collapse of the economy, but instead they may have functioned as external constraints on the regime's discretionary authority, indirectly prompting welfare-enhancing policy adjustments. While the evidence for this second claim is more tentative and should be interpreted with caution, it highlights a mechanism that has not been explored on the literature on sanctions and merits further research. This theory would also be consistent with regime demands for sanction relief despite the stabilization of economic outcomes after sanctions: By constraining discretionary authority and rents, sanctions cornered the regime into an uncomfortable and unstable position, forcing it to implement welfare-enhancing policy reforms while bargaining electoral conditions for relaxed constraints.

The implications of the analysis and conclusions reached by this Element are consequential for the debate over sanctions on Venezuela. While sanctions may have failed to deliver regime change, neither did they precipitate the collapse of the economy or further deterioration of Venezuelans' living standards. On the contrary, by constraining the regime's room for maneuver, sanctions may have compelled limited reforms that yielded modest welfare gains. The Maduro government's consistent demand for sanction relief in every negotiation over electoral conditions further underscores their relevance: While democratization remains elusive, sanctions appear to have functioned as leverage for incremental democratic concessions, and - perhaps unintendedly - as a catalyst for some material relief.

[3] This possibility seems remote, given Venezuela's track record with exchange controls as a mechanism to distribute oil rents. In the thirty-five years spanning from 1983 to 2019, Venezuela has been subject to exchange controls for twenty-six, having undergone long periods of rigid exchange controls: Regimen Cambiario Diferencial (RECADI) from 1983 to 1989; Oficina Tecnica de Administración Cambiaria (OTAC) from 1994 to 1996; and the Comisión Nacional de Administración de Divisas (CADIVI) created by Hugo Chavez in 2003, and extending for more than seventeen years up until 2020. For more details on Venezuela exchange control regimes see (Reinhart and Santos, 2016) and (Bahar et al., 2018).

## 2 Timeline of Economic Events

Venezuela's economic collapse began by mid 2013, when shortages of basic goods such as food and household staples became widespread and living standards deteriorated sharply. By early 2014, the country was already facing a deepening macroeconomic crisis–marked by worsening food scarcity and mounting political repression – which was later compounded by a sharp decline in global oil prices that would halve Venezuela's export revenues by 2015 (IMF, 2015; Santos, 2017, 2021). By every comparative measure, Venezuela went on to experience the largest economic collapse in modern history outside of war or natural disaster. Writing about the GDP loss recorded just between 2014 and 2016, a cumulative contraction of 25.2%, Barrios and Santos (2017) conclude:

> *In the last twenty years, only four three-year periods worldwide have recorded greater economic devastation: Libya (−60.5% between 2009–2011), South Sudan (−45.9% between 2010–2012), Iraq (−36.2% between 2001–2003), and the Central African Republic (−35.5% between 2012–2014). In all these cases, the collapse coincided with armed conflicts of various kinds, which makes the Venezuelan episode a truly exceptional case of economic ruin.*[4]

Policy decisions under Maduro's government further deepened the crisis, pushing the country into a prolonged cycle of hyperinflation and contraction. Venezuela suffered an additional 15.7% loss of economic activity in 2017, and hyperinflation officially began in December of that year when monthly inflation surpassed the 50% threshold (55.6%).

In total, the country lost 74% of its GDP between 2013 and 2020. Half of that contraction occurred between 2013 and 2017, and two-thirds took place before the imposition of sanctions on the state-owned oil company Petroleos de Venezuela (PDVSA) in January 2019. The oil industry mirrored the evolution of GDP, losing 79% of its output between 2013 and 2020. A quarter of that loss occurred between 2013 and 2017, and more than half was recorded before the January 2019 sanctions. By 2016 Venezuela's debt had surpassed the $120 billion mark and its ratio to exports (4.37) was the highest among all the countries covered in the World Development Indicators database of the World Bank that year. As documented by Bahar et al. (2019), Venezuela's sovereign risk averaged 2,364 basis points (or 23.64%) from January to August 2017 and did not significantly depart from those levels once financial sanctions were imposed later that month. Spreads skyrocketed more than a month later, once the

[4] Barrios and Santos (2017), p. 92.

Venezuelan debt entered in outright default in November of that year after a failed meeting convened by the Venezuelan government with creditors in Caracas.

As reported by Hernández and Monaldi (2016), the Venezuelan oil industry was already in a state of profound financial and operational fragility in 2016. Net cash-generating exports had eroded to nearly half of reported production, once the subsidized domestic market, and in-kind debt repayments to China were discounted. At the same time, PDVSA faced a crushing fiscal burden, as resources were systematically diverted to social programs and extra-budgetary funds, while debt service costs escalated amid restricted access to credit markets. Mounting arrears to service contractors led major international firms to curtail operations, exacerbating technical bottlenecks, while chronic power outages, refinery accidents, and shortages of inputs undermined reliability across the supply chain. Inflation, exchange-rate distortions, and the bloated payroll further inflated costs, pushing the company's cash flow into persistent deficit.

By 2020, Venezuela's level of economic activity had fallen back to that of 1964, with income per capita levels not seen since the 1940s (World Bank, 2021). The Venezuelan exodus had reached, by mid 2019, approximately 3.9 million people or 14% of its total population[5]. It has been estimated at 7.9 million people or 24% of its population by 2024.[6] Thus, it has become the largest population displacement recorded in Latin America, and among the largest in the world together with Syria, Afghanistan, and, more recently, Ukraine.[7]

## *Financial Sanctions and Democratic Backsliding*

On March 8, 2015, President Barack Obama signed Executive Order 13692, imposing targeted sanctions on eleven senior current or former Venezuelan officials, citing corruption and human rights violations (White House, 2015). Later that year, the opposition coalition won a decisive victory in the parliamentary elections of December 6, 2015, securing a two-thirds supermajority in the National Assembly for the first time since Hugo Chávez came to power seventeen years earlier. However, the pro-government Supreme Court of Justice (TSJ) swiftly blocked four opposition deputies from Amazonas state from taking office, citing alleged irregularities in the electoral process that it claimed affected the validity of the vote in that region (TSJ, 2015, 2016a). By excluding

[5] (UNHCR, 2019)
[6] (UNHCR, 2025)
[7] (for Refugees, UNHCR)

these deputies, the ruling deprived the opposition of the qualified majority needed to override presidential vetoes, appoint or remove key officials, and pass constitutional reforms independently. In April 2016, the TSJ formally declared the National Assembly in contempt and nullified its legislative powers (TSJ, 2016b). Later that year, when the opposition launched a recall referendum effort to remove Maduro, the TSJ and National Electoral Council (CNE) suspended the process (BBC News, 2016).

By March 2017, the TSJ escalated its attack on the legislature, dissolving the National Assembly entirely (TSJ, 2017). This decision triggered a massive wave of protests throughout the country. Heavy repression from security forces left 157 people dead, 2000 people injured and more than 5000 imprisoned (Llorens, 2018). Moreover, President Maduro called elections for a parallel Constitutional Assembly (ANC), tasked with drafting a new constitution. The ANC election, which was called for without meeting the necessary constitutional requirements, was held on July 30, 2017, amid nationwide protests and international condemnation (TalCual Digital, 2019).

In response, the Trump administration issued Executive Order 13808 on August 25, 2017, imposing financial sanctions that barred the Venezuelan government and its state-owned oil company (PDVSA) from issuing new bonds in United States' markets or trading existing bonds there, effectively preventing both entities from refinancing their external debt (U.S. Treasury, 2017). These were financial sanctions and did not prohibit oil trade between the United States and Venezuela. Soon after, the European Union imposed its own targeted sanctions (EU Council Decision, 2017). Another significant development was the formation of the Grupo de Lima, a multilateral coalition of Latin American countries and Canada, established in August 2017 in response to the ANC with the explicit purpose of coordinating diplomatic pressure to restore democratic order in Venezuela. Following this, later in November 2017, Nicolas Maduro appointed Manuel Quevedo, a high-ranking official of the National Guard to head PDVSA, effectively militarizing the oil company. He was president of PDVSA and Minister of Oil until 2020.

## Constitutional Crisis and "Oil" Sanctions

Despite widespread international rejection, the Maduro regime proceeded with presidential elections on May 20, 2018, which were broadly denounced as fraudulent due to bans on opposition candidates, electoral manipulation, and widespread irregularities. The elections had the lowest turnout for a presidential election in the history of Venezuela, regardless of the source: 46.1% according to the Venezuelan Electoral Council (Venezuelan Electoral Council, 2021),

25.1% according to the Mesa de la Unidad Democrática,[8] 17.3% according to independent pollsters (HuffPost, 2018). Considering that the essential tenets of credible, transparent, and inclusive elections were violated in the electoral process, the international democratic community rejected the process and did not recognize its results, including the European Union (Parliament, 2018), the Organization of American States (Organization of American States, 2021), the Grupo de Lima (Grupo de Lima, 2018), as well as the United States (Reuters, 2018). Only a handful of countries – including China, Cuba, Iran, Russia, Syria, and Turkey – recognized the election result (Infobae, 2018).

When Maduro's second term formally expired on January 10, 2019, the opposition-led National Assembly, pursuant to its authority under the Venezuelan constitution to fill a vacancy in the presidency, appointed the President of the legislative body, Juan Guaidó, as the Interim President of Venezuela. On February 5 the National Assembly passed the Statute Governing the Transition to Democracy to reestablish the Validity of the Constitution of the Bolivarian Republic of Venezuela, a bill that "governs the installation of a provisional Government and the call to free elections," and "establishes the election of new rectors of the National Electoral Council, new magistrates of the Supreme Tribunal of Justice and new representatives of the Citizen Power" (Asamblea Nacional, 2019).

On January 23, the United States recognized Juan Guaidó as Interim President of Venezuela (U.S. Department of State, 2019). Canada followed shortly (Global Affairs Canada, 2019) as well as more than half of the twenty-eight European Union countries, including Germany, France, Spain, and the United Kingdom (BBC News, 2019a).

On January 28 2019, the US Treasury's Office of Foreign Assets Control (OFAC) designated PDVSA under Executive Order 13850, freezing its assets under the US jurisdiction and prohibiting its citizens from engaging in transactions with PDVSA. The measure effectively banned imports of Venezuelan crude into the United States and restricted the export of refined products and diluents critical for processing heavy crude (U.S. Department of the Treasury).

In parallel, OFAC issued General License 8, which allowed Chevron, Halliburton, Schlumberger, Baker Hughes, and Weatherford International to continue "ordinary and necessary" activities with PDVSA to preserve assets and maintain operations. This authorization, repeatedly renewed through 2019,

[8] The umbrella organization used by the Venezuelan opposition in the 2015 National Assembly election, where the opposition won two-thirds of the seats, formed by parties and leaders banned from the 2018 presidential election.

essentially permitted United States' firms to sustain the status quo of existing contracts but not to expand or modify them (Hernández, 2022).

By the end of February 2019, thirty-six countries had recognized Juan Guaidó as Interim President, a figure that grew to more than fifty by the end of that year (Foreign Policy, 2019). That same month, Venezuela suffered a series of nationwide blackouts, including the longest power outage in the country's history, which left most of the population without electricity for nearly a week and caused persistent supply disruptions for months afterward (Reuters, 2019; BBC News, 2019b).[9]

Amid worsening conditions, Juan Guaidó and other opposition leaders attempted to rally military support for a transition of power on April 30, 2019, but the effort failed and forced many opposition figures into exile (BBC News, 2019c). Later that year, on August 5, 2019, the Trump administration issued Executive Order 13884, imposing a comprehensive embargo that effectively froze all Venezuelan government assets under US jurisdiction, blocked the Central Bank of Venezuela's access to dollars, and prohibited nearly all transactions with officials of the Maduro regime (White House, 2019).

## *COVID and Relief of Sanctions*

The onset of the COVID-19 pandemic in 2020 further deepened Venezuela's economic crisis. From 2020 onward, sanctions expanded to include third-country intermediaries that helped market Venezuelan crude. In April 2020, with the issuance of General License 8F, permissions previously granted to maintain the status quo were significantly curtailed: Chevron and others were restricted to the limited rights of minority shareholders in joint ventures, barred from financing PDVSA's share of investments, distributing dividends (even in crude), or receiving oil in payment of debt. Companies could still cover basic costs such as local taxes, utilities, and salaries, but new investment and debt arrangements were prohibited. These restrictions shifted the burden of financing entirely to PDVSA, which lacked the capacity to sustain capital expenditures, and were subsequently reiterated in renewed licenses through 2022 (BBC News, 2019c).

---

[9] General License 8 was renewed on multiple occasions: 8A (June 2019), 8B (July 2019), 8C (August 2019), 8D (October 2019), 8E (January 2020), 8F (April 2020), 8G (November 2020), 8H (October 2021), 8I (November 2021, expired June 2022), and 8J (May 2022 - maintaining the same restrictions until Chevron's limited authorization was revised again in late 2022. For a detailed discussion of the scope and implications of the General Licenses that granted Chevron and US contractors varying degrees of operational maneuver in Venezuela, see Hernández (2022).

In April, the United States' Department of Justice indicted Nicolás Maduro and senior officials on charges of narco-terrorism and corruption, offering a reward of up to $15 million for information leading to Maduro's arrest (U.S. DOJ, 2020). In June, the Treasury imposed additional sanctions designating four shipping companies for operating vessels that transported Iranian oil products to Venezuela in violation of sanctions and embargoes, attempting to cut off critical gasoline imports essential to the country's economy (U.S. Treasury, 2020). These measures marked the final phase of the Trump administration's "maximum pressure" strategy: Imposing sanctions on nearly every economic sector in the expectation that mounting constraints would either force a democratic transition or provide leverage for negotiations.

Amid tightening sanctions and worsening economic conditions, the Venezuelan government organized elections for a new National Assembly on December 6, 2020. Major opposition parties and leaders boycotted the vote, denouncing it as illegitimate due to restrictions on political participation, lack of electoral guarantees, and manipulation by the pro-government National Electoral Council (CNE). In its final report, the European External Action Service (EEAS) concluded that the process failed to meet international democratic standards and reaffirmed that the 2015-elected National Assembly remained the only legitimate parliamentary body (European Council, 2020). Following the vote, the United States also rejected the results and reaffirmed its support for the opposition-led Assembly (U.S. Department of State, 2020). In 2021, Venezuela continued to face severe humanitarian hardship and renewed political tensions. Early that year, the European Union announced that it would no longer formally recognize opposition leader Juan Guaidó as Venezuela's interim president, though it reiterated that Nicolás Maduro's 2018 reelection remained illegitimate (Euronews, 2021). In November, regional elections were held, marking the opposition's return to electoral participation after years of boycotts. Despite this reengagement, independent observers and opposition figures reported widespread irregularities and structural advantages for pro-government candidates (European Union Election Observation Mission, 2021). The year closed with initial steps toward renewed negotiations between the opposition and the government, first mediated by Norway and later culminating in the Barbados Agreement framework.

In October 2022, the Biden administration offered a limited relaxation of sanctions by granting Chevron Corporation a specific license to resume restricted oil production and export operations in Venezuela, under clear conditions tied to political concessions. This was the first significant easing of sanctions since they were imposed in 2017 and 2019. Through General License No.41, Chevron was authorized to produce oil but not to pay taxes or royalties directly to the Maduro government, aiming to ensure funds were ring-fenced for debt repayment and humanitarian uses (U.S. Treasury, 2022). In return, the Maduro administration agreed to allow the opposition to hold primary elections to select its leadership and ultimately enable the candidacy of María Corina Machado for the 2024 presidential election.

Throughout 2023, diplomatic tensions continued, marked by a cycle of temporary concessions and renewed repression. In October, the United States temporarily lifted key sanctions on Venezuela's oil, gas, and gold sectors after the signing of the Barbados Agreement, making this relief conditional on Nicolás Maduro's commitments to release political prisoners and allow internationally monitored free and fair elections. This easing took the form of General License No.44, which authorized to resume certain transactions with PDVSA and the Venezuelan mining sector for a limited period (U.S. Treasury, 2023). However, by November Maduro's government backtracked on these commitments when security forces arrested multiple members of opposition leader María Corina Machado's campaign team, drawing condemnation from the United States and the European Union for undermining the agreed electoral guarantees.

In December 2023, the United States warned that it would reimpose sanctions if the Maduro regime failed to fulfill its commitments under the Barbados Agreement, highlighting the fragility of the diplomatic framework and Maduro's ongoing reluctance to implement meaningful democratic reforms. Ultimately, General License No.44 expired in April 2024 after the regime failed to meet its core conditions, which included allowing free and fair elections and respecting opposition candidates' right to run. Instead, authorities upheld a ban preventing María Corina Machado from standing as a presidential candidate, and subsequently barred her chosen substitute, Corina Yoris, from registering as well (U.S. Department of State, 2024). Under mounting domestic and international pressure, Maduro eventually conceded by permitting opposition figure Edmundo González Urrutia to stand as a unity candidate – but this sequence of obstructions triggered the wind-down and nonrenewal of the license (U.S. Treasury, 2024).

### Presidential Elections and Return of Sanctions

The political situation deteriorated significantly in 2024. After Nicolás Maduro failed to fulfill his commitments under the Barbados Agreement, the United States reinstated sanctions on Venezuela's vital oil and gas sector in April 2024, restoring financial pressure on PDVSA and associated state revenues (U.S. Treasury, 2024). In July, the presidential election was marred by widespread allegations of fraud, voter intimidation, and ballot manipulation. Despite independently corroborated evidence indicating that opposition candidate Edmundo González Urrutia won by a significant margin – with estimates suggesting he secured around 70% of the vote – Maduro refused to acknowledge defeat and declared himself the winner (U.S. Mission to the OAS, 2024; U.S. Department of State, 2024). The outcome was swiftly rejected by international election observers, the European Union, the United States, and multiple Latin American governments, all of whom cited severe irregularities and the absence of democratic guarantees (European External Action Service, 2024).

## 3 Critical Literature Review

As discussed in the introduction, the evolution of key economic and developmental outcomes around sanctions seems to contradict the punitive narrative that sanctions acted as collective punishment on Venezuelans. Given this contradiction, it is important to critically assess how such a narrative has been both substantiated and rebutted. In this section, we now discuss the literature assessing the developmental effects of United States' sanctions on Venezuela. First, we outline the scope of our review and present the list of contributions covered – both supportive and critical of the view that sanctions collectively punished Venezuelans. We then discuss the literature chronologically, showing how different contributions address each other. Finally, we conclude this section outlining the three key gaps in the literature favoring the notion of sanctions-as-collective-punishment.

### *Scope of This Literature Review*

The scope of this review is deliberately focused on contributions that meet two specific criteria. First, we concentrate on studies analyzing the impact of sanctions on Venezuela following their implementation in 2017. While the broader sanctions literature includes numerous cross-country analyses and studies of other sanctioned regimes, we consider only those that advance Venezuela-specific analyses. This targeted approach allows us to assess the evidence base regarding this particular case, which has been the subject of scholarly and policy debate.

Second, we limit our focus to quantitative contributions that employ methodological frameworks to estimate the causal effects of these sanctions. These studies share a common feature: They attempt to construct "counterfactual" benchmarks – estimates of what would have happened to economic and development outcomes in the absence of sanctions – to isolate the sanctions' impact from other factors affecting Venezuela's economy. This approach distinguishes the literature we review from a broader set of policy notes, legal analyses, and opinion pieces that discuss Venezuela sanctions from normative or descriptive perspectives without attempting to estimate causal effects through quantitative, causal approximations.

It should be noted that the literature that meets these criteria varies in terms of methodological rigor and publication status. As of the writing of this Element, only one paper in this list has undergone peer review in an academic journal. Other contributions exist as academic working papers, policy analyses, or opinion pieces released by think tanks, media outlets, or individual researchers. This variation in publication status requires careful consideration when assessing the robustness and reliability of findings across the literature. Finally, while several other articles and books quote or reintroduce the arguments and findings presented in the contributions discussed next, we limit our focus to the main sources of the analytic findings used to weigh on the debate of Venezuelan sanctions as collective punishment.[10]

## *Summary of the Literature*

Table 1 outlines the contributions providing quantitative evidence in favor of the view that US sanctions on Venezuela worked as a tool for collective punishment, while Table 2 outlines contributions providing evidence rejecting that view.

### *The "Causal Chain": 2017 Sanctions, Oil Production, and Venezuela's Collapse*

The first contribution formally studying the effects of Venezuelan sanctions was Rodríguez (2018). In this study, released by the Washington Office on Latin America (WOLA), Rodríguez argues that the 2017 financial sanctions caused a reduction in Venezuelan oil production. Rodríguez argues that changes in oil production observed in Colombia provide an adequate counterfactual of what would have happened to Venezuelan oil production had the 2017 financial sanctions not been enacted. Chiefly, both Venezuela and Colombia saw a decline in production after oil prices fell under the $30 per barrel threshold -which the author argues would be expected in both countries given their reliance on costly extraction of extra-heavy oils. However, Venezuelan oil

10 A few of the contributions quoting the studies discussed in our literature review are Rodríguez (2021, 2022a, 2022d, 2023, 2024, 2025a).

**Table 1** Studies supporting the "sanctions as collective punishment" viewpoint

| Title | Authors | Type | Institution | Summary |
|---|---|---|---|---|
| Crude Realities: Understanding Venezuela's Economic Collapse | Rodríguez (2018) | Policy Analysis | WOLA | Identifies that Venezuela's economy collapsed due to a decline in oil production, which accelerated after the 2017 financial sanctions. Compares Venezuelan and Colombian oil production trends to argue sanctions contributed to economic decline. |
| Punishing Civilians: United States Sanctions on Venezuela | Sachs and Weisbrot (2019) | Opinion Article | Challenge | Argues sanctions caused significant humanitarian impacts including 40,000 deaths in 2017–2018. Claims sanctions prevented debt restructuring and caused oil production collapse, cutting off essential imports. |
| Sanctions and the Venezuelan Economy: What the Data Say | Rodríguez (2019) | Working Paper | Torino Economics | Using synthetic control methods and cross-country comparisons, estimates financial sanctions caused losses of $16.9 billion per year in oil revenue. |
| Impacto de las Sanciones Financieras y Petroleras sobre la Economía Venezolana | Oliveros (2020) | Policy Analysis | WOLA | Shows oil production in Venezuela after the 2017 sanctions underperformed pre-treatment trends. |
| Sanctions and Imports of Essential Goods: A Closer Look at the Equipo Anova (2021) Results | Rodríguez (2022b) | Working Paper | Self | Critiques Equipo Anova (2021) findings, demonstrating their conclusions about sanctions improving imports resulted from data errors and methodological flaws. Finds no evidence that sanctions improved imports of essential goods. |

| | | | | |
|---|---|---|---|---|
| Sanctions and Oil Production: Evidence from Venezuela's Orinoco Basin | Rodríguez (2022c) | Journal Article | Latin American Economic Review | Uses firm-level data to show the 2017 financial sanctions caused greater oil production losses in firms with pre-sanctions access to credit. Estimates sanctions explain about half of production losses, with impact of $6.2 billion annually. |
| Why Economic Sanctions Backfire: The Role of Emigration in the Venezuelan Case | Idrobo (2024) | Working Paper | Self | Examines how sanctions may strengthen authoritarian regimes by triggering emigration of political opposition supporters. Uses Venezuelan case to show opponents of the regime were more likely to migrate after sanctions. |
| Sanctions and Venezuelan Migration | Rodríguez (2025b) | Working Paper | Self | Analyzes relationship between sanctions and Venezuelan emigration flows. Argues that by worsening economic conditions, sanctions contributed to the massive exodus of Venezuelans, creating humanitarian challenges in receiving countries. |

**Table 2** Studies rejecting the “sanctions as collective punishment” viewpoint

| Title | Authors | Type | Institution | Summary |
|---|---|---|---|---|
| Don’t Blame Washington for Venezuela’s Oil Woes: A Rebuttal | Hausmann and Muci (2019) | Opinion Article | Americas Quarterly | Argues Venezuela’s economic crisis predated sanctions, and that the 2019 oil output decline was caused by electrical blackouts, not sanctions. Questions whether Colombia is an appropriate counterfactual for Venezuela’s oil production trends. |
| Sanciones: ¿causa o consecuencia de la crisis? | Morales-Arilla (2019) | Opinion Article | Prodavinci | Contends Venezuela’s oil production decline was primarily caused by militarization of the oil industry and corruption investigations, not sanctions. Notes production was declining before sanctions due to mismanagement and investment cuts. |
| Impact of the 2017 Sanctions on Venezuela: Revisiting the Evidence | Bahar et al. (2019) | Policy Analysis | Brookings Institution | Challenges the causal link between sanctions and humanitarian crisis, showing social indicators were declining before sanctions. Argues Venezuela had already lost access to capital markets prior to sanctions, making financial sanctions redundant. |
| Impacto de las Sanciones Financieras Internacionales contra Venezuela: Nueva Evidencia | Zambrano et al. (2021) | Policy Analysis | ANOVA | Claims financial sanctions were associated with improvements in imports of food and medicines, while acknowledging negative effects on oil production. Suggests sanctions may have forced positive policy changes including economic liberalization by the government. |
| Sanctions on Venezuela Are Not Driving Migration to the US Southwest Border: An Empirical Assessment | Bahar and Hausmann (2025) | Working Paper | Center for Global Development | Finds higher oil income and prices correlate with more Venezuelan migration to the United States, not less. Argues sanctions actually reduce migration flows by constraining economic activity, contradicting claims that sanctions worsen the migration crisis. |

production collapsed after financial sanctions were enacted in August 2017, while Colombian production remained steady.

Rodríguez (2018) first introduced what we call the "causal chain" behind the argument that sanctions induced the collapse of the Venezuelan economy. By eroding oil production, sanctions limited Venezuela's oil export revenues, which constrained the country's import capabilities, producing the collapse of the economy: "I argue that Venezuela's economy has imploded because it can't import, and it can't import because its export revenue has collapsed." This argument is most drastically presented in Sachs and Weisbrot (2019). After reasserting the findings in Rodríguez (2018), Sachs and Weisbrot extend the implications of the causal chain to argue that by "ending much of the country's access to these essential imports including medicine and food," the 2017 financial sanctions induced the death of 40,000 Venezuelans. Chiefly, the way the authors estimate such effects is by assuming that the increase in mortality rates in Venezuela between 2017 and 2018 was fully a consequence of the 2017 sanctions: "there was a 31 percent increase in general mortality from 2017 to 2018. This would imply an increase of more than 40,000 deaths." While this and other similarly calculated estimates would be extensively cited in policy and political debates regarding the effects of sanctions (Fox News, 2019; RealClearPolitics, 2019), Sachs would later say that "I don't want anyone to think that there is precision in these numbers" (Democracy Now!, 2019).

At least three other contributions introduced further evidence in favor of the view that the 2017 sanctions eroded Venezuela's oil production - and extrapolated these findings to argue that sanctions were the key culprit behind the collapse of the Venezuelan economy. Rodríguez (2019), released by Torino Economics, leveraged the synthetic control methodology to produce a data-driven counterfactual of what the Venezuelan oil production would have been had the 2017 sanctions not been enacted. The paper argues that sanctions led to a decrease in oil production of 797,000 barrels of oil per day, adding to lost oil export revenue of $16.9 billion per year. Chiefly, the paper underscores the "causal chain" argument:

> If one assumes that large variations in mortality (particularly increases, which are rare) are driven by changes in income and one assumes that Venezuelan GDP would have stabilized in the absence of the decline in production caused by the 2017 sanctions, then one can conclude that the main cause of the increase in mortality that year was the adoption of sanctions.

Similarly, Oliveros (2020) argues that there was an acceleration in the collapse of oil production after the enactment of the 2017 financial sanctions. The analysis uses monthly drops in pre-sanctions productions levels between 1% and 2% as a counterfactual range to calculate the effect of sanctions on oil export revenues, estimating a drop in revenues of $31 billion to $17.5 billion between August 2017 and July 2020. Now again, the analysis advances the "causal chain" discussed earlier: "With the fall of oil production in Venezuela, the Venezuelan government's foreign exchange revenues also drop, producing an import contraction that, ultimately, affects the poorest Venezuelans."

Finally, Rodríguez (2022c) presents the only piece of independently peer-reviewed evidence that the 2017 sanctions affected oil production. Published in the *Latin American Economic* Review,[11] the paper uses production data from different firms within Venezuela's Orinoco Oil Basin. Leveraging a difference-in-differences framework, the paper finds that oil production dropped faster for firms with better pre-sanctions access to financing after the 2017 financial sanctions, which limited PDVSA's access to US financial markets.[12] Despite being peer-reviewed, the paper has been criticized on methodological grounds. Among other criticisms, Bahar (2024) discusses the paper's main figure to make the point that firms with and without PDVSA financing agreements were clearly in different production trends before sanctions were first enacted, rendering the fundamental assumption of difference-in-difference designs (parallel trends between treatment and control units) implausible to estimate causal effects in this setting. In any event, as the paper concludes Rodríguez (2022c) reemphasizes the "causal chain" of the collective punishment argument: "the evidence suggests that financial sanctions can and did act as an economic surgical strike capable of replicating the effects of a full-fledged trade embargo."

### *Initial Rebuttals: Did These Papers Prove That Sanctions Eroded Oil Production?*

The release of Rodríguez (2018) and Sachs and Weisbrot (2019) produced an initial set of rebuttals on whether these findings proved that the 2017 financial sanctions eroded oil production and overall living standards in Venezuela. First, Hausmann and Muci (2019) questioned the validity of using Colombian oil production as a counterfactual for what would have happened to Venezuelan oil production in the absence of sanctions. The authors argue that Venezuela and Colombia were on diverging production trends before sanctions. Moreover, they argue that oil production drops in Venezuela between January 2016 and August 2017 were concentrated in oil fields with light and medium oils, so oil production in Venezuela did not fall during that period because of oil price drops - as was the case in Colombia. The authors argue

[11] The CiteScore rankings for the Latin American Policy Journal can be found at www.scopus.com/sourceid/21100401085.

[12] *Petroleos de Venezuela, Sociedad Anónima* (PDVSA) is Venezuela's National Oil Company.

that Venezuela's share of oil production from OPEC countries had been falling at similar rates since 1999.

Morales-Arilla (2019) seconds the argument that Colombia provides an inadequate counterfactual, underscoring that oil prices quickly recovered and were already above the $30 per barrel benchmark by May 2016, so they cannot explain the pre-sanctions drops in oil production in Venezuela. Citing Bloomberg (2016), the article references consulting firms in the Venezuelan oil sector arguing that pre-sanctions production drops extended to lighter oils whose production should not remain commercially viable at lower oil prices. Consultants argued that the key reasons for pre-sanctions production declines were "drilling challenges, natural gas compression issues and well maintenance difficulties due to restriction of field services and theft," not lower oil prices. The author argues that 76% of all Venezuelan oil production losses between 2015 and 2018 either occurred before the August 2017 sanctions or could be explained by extrapolating pre-sanctions production trends.[13]

Morales-Arilla (2019) also makes the point that assuming that worsening post-sanctions trends are a consequence of sanctions would be confounding concurrent treatments. This would be especially so given how sanctions were triggered by the enactment of the Constitutional Assembly of 2017, a massive institutional shock that could have induced further production drops regardless of sanctions. Moreover, the author argues that the imposition of military control over the oil industry, which followed shortly after the enactment of the 2017 financial sanctions, could have explained further disruptions to oil production, as shown anecdotally in Reuters (2018a). The author argues that the multiplicity of relevant treatments occurring in Venezuela during this narrow period of time makes the use of synthetic control specifications inadequate for the study of the potential effects of sanctions on oil production, preemptively rebutting the validity of later findings presented in Rodríguez (2019).

Perhaps most important in the list of initial rebuttals, Bahar et al. (2019) extend the scope of criticisms beyond events in the oil sector. Released by the Brookings Institution, the authors first make the point that the financial nature of the 2017 sanctions did not erode Venezuela's access to international financial markets, because such access was already closed to Venezuela due to the country's insolvency - a point also raised by Hausmann and Muci (2019).

[13] Interestingly, Chart 7 in Rodríguez (2019) shows that the difference in oil production between Venezuela and its synthetic counterfactual goes from statistically significant positive values in late 2015 to statistically significant negative values at the time that sanctions were enacted. This is consistent with the pre-sanctions drop in Venezuelan oil production that Rodríguez (2018) and Sachs and Weisbrot (2019) impute to low oil prices, which is rebutted by Hausmann and Muci (2019) and Morales-Arilla (2019).

One way to see this is through the fact that the imposition of sanctions was not followed by an increase in the country's sovereign risk, which by that point was already 9.5 times the risk premium paid on average by emerging markets. The article then provides further evidence against the view that pre-sanctions drops in oil production were driven by low oil prices in 2016, but due to managerial factors that continued -or possibly worsened- once sanctions were enacted. That is, it is impossible to disentangle pre-sanctions trends from the effects of sanctions. Chiefly, the article extends this logic to key socioeconomic development outcomes to challenge Sachs and Weisbrot's (2019) claim that sanctions "inflicted . . . more than 40,000 deaths from 2017–2018." As mentioned earlier, this estimate is based on the assumption that mortality increases in this period were strictly a consequence of the 2017 financial sanctions. However, the paper shows that imports of food and medicines, infant mortality rates, and the caloric purchasing power of the country's minimum wage were all in deep negative and worsening trends by the time that sanctions were first enacted. According to the authors, this means both that post-sanctions events cannot be plausibly disentangled from pre-sanctions trends, and that the bulk of the deterioration in living standards discussed in Sachs and Weisbrot (2019) preceded -and hence cannot be attributed to- the 2017 financial sanctions.

### *Critiques on the Causal Chain: Effects of Sanctions on Essential Imports.*

By this point, studies had focused on the potential effects of sanctions on oil production, or lack thereof. However, the argument extending contested evidence on oil production to the collapse of the Venezuelan economy and of Venezuelans' living standards is implicitly based on a separate logic. As mentioned earlier, the logical "causal chain" underlying the reasoning of Venezuelan sanctions as collective punishment travels through alleged restrictions to the country's current account: Dwindling oil production leads to a reduction in oil export revenues, which in turn limits the country's capabilities of importing essential goods -especially food and medicines. Sanctions-induced scarcity of these imported basic staples is the main culprit behind the collapse in the country's living standards, the argument goes.

While Bahar et al. (2019) emphasized the drastic collapse in imports and living standards before financial sanctions were first enacted, it did not discuss how these variables evolved after the sanctions. The first paper to explicitly consider the question of whether sanctions induced a collapse in the country's import capabilities through quantitative causal methodologies was Zambrano et al. (2021). Released by Anova Policy Research, the article used a regression discontinuity design to evaluate whether monthly food and medicine imports dropped discretely at the time of sanctions. Interestingly, despite estimating a negative effect of sanctions on oil production through this methodology, the authors find a *positive* effect of sanctions on these essential imports.

How could imports increase if oil production/exports decreased? Zambrano et al. (2021) presented the first iteration of the hypothesis that we outline later in this Element. Sanctions coincided with the government's first steps towards de facto liberalize internal prices and foreign exchange rates. While this might have been a coincidence, the authors say that "it is possible to argue that the change in the government's policy orientation, which ultimately led to the relaxation of the framework of controls, was also an immediate consequence of the tightening of financial sanctions against PDVSA. In this case, the greater external availability of food and medicine would be a consequence of the sanctions policy, at least indirectly."

The specific statistical results of this analysis' regression discontinuity specifications would be contested on technical grounds. Specifically, in a self-released working paper, Rodríguez (2022b) argues that the conclusions in Zambrano et al. (2021) are contingent on coding errors, specific regression specification and outcome variable transformation choices, and a narrow definition for the set of product codes to be considered food. Interestingly, both papers seem to concur on the finding that there was a positive change in the "slope," that the import collapse stopped (or came to a halt) after sanctions. This makes sense from the perspective of Bahar et al. (2019): Once imports had collapsed so aggressively before sanctions, it was essentially impossible for them to continue falling at similar rates. This key fact is often absent from the literature: Most of the economic collapse preceded the sanctions.

This is something that Zambrano (2023) reconsiders in the context of the 2019 oil sanctions, in a "thread" only released on Twitter/X. While the aforementioned papers show that imports of food and medicines stabilized after the 2017 financial sanctions, these essential imports started to increase after the 2019 oil sanctions. While it could be argued that such improvements could have been bigger in the absence of sanctions, it is hard to look at these facts and argue that both the 2017 and 2019 sanctions led to a collapse in the availability of imported essential goods - a key step in the "causal chain" logic that sanctions worked as a collective punishment on Venezuelans. Most importantly, Zambrano (2023) argues that these changing trends, which have to do with the de facto liberalization and dollarization of the economy, warrant the question of whether the government would have pursued such drastic economic policy reforms in the absence of sanctions. If the relevant economic policy changes were triggered by sanctions, then the corresponding stabilization and improvement in living standards would be a consequence of sanctions.

### *Did Sanctions Cause the Venezuelan Refugee Shock?*

One of the main consequences of Venezuela's economic collapse was the resulting refugee shock that saw 25% of Venezuela's population leave the country, mainly to neighboring countries in South, Central, and North America. A more recent strain of the literature on Venezuelan sanctions has started to focus on whether sanctions were the main culprit behind the Venezuelan exodus.

A first paper in this literature is Idrobo (2024), who argues that sanctions inadvertently weakened domestic opposition against the Maduro regime because opponents are most likely to choose to "exit" in response to worsening economic conditions (Hirschman, 1970). The paper takes data from Venezuelans' social security records capturing the year when individuals stop participating in the system. Arguing that this metric is a proxy for individuals' migration choices, the author shows that migration after 2017 was strongest in areas with higher baseline opposition support.[14]

A second paper in this literature is Rodríguez (2025b). While not presenting original results based on quantitative causal inference methods, this article reaffirms the "causal chain" logic described earlier and leverages prior evidence on the alleged effects of sanctions on oil production to assert that sanctions explain "approximately half of the decline in living standards observed since 2012." Based on this claim and on cross-country analysis of the connection between growth and migration, the author builds migration estimates for different sanction "scenarios" under the new Trump administration. Despite not studying the effects of prior sanctions on the Venezuelan refugee shock, the article estimates that a return to a "Maximum Pressure" sanctions strategy by the Trump administration would lead to an additional one million Venezuelan migrants.

Released by the Center for Global Development (CGD), Bahar and Hausmann (2025) respond to Rodríguez (2025b) arguing that the latter's approach "fails to account for confounding variables that could influence both economic performance and migration simultaneously, such as political repression and institutional deterioration," and "ignores the fact that much of Venezuela's economic decline proceeded the 2017 sanctions." Leveraging methods for time-series analyses, the authors study the association between Venezuelans' outmigration trends and potential Venezuelan oil revenues as an

[14] We provide a critique of Idrobo (2024) in the following subsection.

inverse proxy for the imposition of sanctions. Interestingly, the authors find that higher oil prices and income are associated with an increase in the number of Venezuelans crossing illegally into the United States. The authors argue that this at first counterintuitive finding can be explained by oil revenues allowing Venezuelans to accumulate resources to face the fixed cost of migration, and by oil revenues helping the Maduro regime stabilize its ruling coalition, eroding Venezuelans' hopes for regime change.[15]

## *Are Claims of Sanctions as "Collective Punishment" on Venezuelans Warranted by This Evidence?*

The papers discussed earlier account for the causal quantitative literature on the effects of sanctions on the Venezuelan economy. We first described an initial set of studies documenting effects of sanctions on oil production, and how those studies were contested on different grounds. We then discussed how there is a dearth of evidence that sanctions worsened access to imported essential goods and developmental outcomes, including mortality and migration. Interestingly, there is evidence in favor of the view that the collapse in imports stopped after the 2017 sanctions, and started to recover after the 2019 sanctions. We believe this point is key: Even if oil production was indeed affected by sanctions, the lack of evidence that sanctions led to a collapse in essential imports, and the evidence that import access actually improved after sanctions, constitutes a fundamental and logical breakdown of the "causal chain" of the sanctions-as-collective-punishment argument.

An important challenge in the literature studying the effects of sanctions on oil production, imports, and other developmental outcomes is the difficulty of disentangling the continuation and worsening of pre-sanctions dynamics eroding the relevant outcomes from the potential effects of sanctions. As discussed in Hausmann and Muci (2019), Morales-Arilla (2019), and Bahar et al. (2019), oil production, essential imports, and developmental outcomes were all in accelerating downward trends before the imposition of financial sanctions in 2017. As these articles argue, it is extremely difficult to conceive a sensible counterfactual for any of the relevant outcomes because no country other than Venezuela has experienced a comparable collapse. In the absence of a plausible counterfactual for what would have happened to Venezuela in any of these

15 The authors acknowledged coding errors in an initial version of this article, but claim that such errors do not alter the articles' broad message: "This note was updated after fixing a minor error in the code that we had previously inadvertently overlooked, resulting in some, but not all, results being different. Our overall conclusions remain the same."

outcomes had sanctions not been enacted, plausible causal effects of sanctions cannot be estimated.

Perhaps most importantly, economic sanctions do not occur in a vacuum, but they are often triggered by meaningful political events and are surrounded by consequential economic events and policy choices. The financial sanctions of 2017 and the oil sanctions of 2019 are no exception. As discussed in the timeline of events, the 2017 sanctions were preceded by the curtailing of legislative prerogatives, the prohibition of a recall referendum in 2016, and by the brutal repression of massive protests and the usurpation of legislative authorities by the *Asamblea Nacional Constituyente* (ANC). Indeed, it was the unconstitutional creation of the ANC which triggered the 2017 sanctions, along with other diplomatic interventions like the *Grupo de Lima*. Finally, they were soon followed by the government's decision to cede managerial control of the oil industry to the Armed Forces, a decision that has been discussed as greatly disruptive for operations in the sector.

Following the imposition of the 2017 financial sanctions, the executive board of PDVSA was restructured and replaced by high-ranking military officials. Reuters (2018a) documents the rise of Manuel Quevedo, a Major General in the Venezuelan National Guard, as president of PDVSA, and his appointment as the Oil Minister of the country. This report from Reuters shows how, a year after his appointment, Quevedo had- from the perspective of industry experts- implemented corrosive reforms which were expected to cause erosions in production. In light of financial sanctions, the constitutional shocks experienced in the country, and the military takeover of the oil industry, all events which may have had an important effects on the oil industry, it is difficult to parse out their specific effects in order to establish causal claims.

This problem of multiple concurrent treatments also plagued the rollout of the 2019 oil sanctions, which were triggered by the start of the constitutional crisis in late January, and were soon followed by the massive blackouts of early March. Independently, each of these concurrent treatments could have plausibly had consequential negative effects on Venezuelan economic and development outcomes in the absence of others. How do we know that the synthetic control findings in Rodríguez (2019) were not a consequence of worsening of pre-sanctions dynamics, or of any of these concurrent events? In Rodríguez (2022c), beyond the lack of parallel pre-treatment trends, which already renders the methodological assumptions of the paper implausible, how do we know that firms with pre-sanctions credit access were not disproportionately exposed to the institutional and operational effects of the Constitutional Assembly and of military control shocks over the oil sector? The fact that all these consequential events occurred in such proximity makes it hard to identify independent causal effects on outcomes that could plausibly be eroded by any of them.

This criticism is even more relevant for Idrobo (2024), who argues that sanctions helped stabilize the Maduro regime by inducing regime opponents to migrate. As a matter of fact, the finding that opposition individuals were more likely to migrate after the start of the Venezuelan economic crisis has been identified in other recent contributions to the migration literature (Cabra-Ruiz et al., 2024; Morales-Arilla et al., 2025). Idrobo (2024) uses individual records and local aggregates of formal labor force participation at a yearly level to proxy for migration. This first methodological decision is already problematic, as people may drop from the formal labor force for economic reasons other than migration. Most importantly, other papers in the literature on migration are careful not to conclude that opponents' exit was driven by a particular separate component of the complex and intertwined political and economic events that plagued Venezuela after 2014.

The reason is that the result could be explained by any of all the meaningful concurrent events. For example, the last year of Idrobo's (2024) pre-treatment period is 2016, a year when the opposition-led legislature was prevented from enacting any laws, and when the opposition was not allowed to pursue a constitutionally enshrined recall referendum on Nicolás Maduro. Moreover, 2017 started with an effort to illegalize the opposition-controlled legislature, which triggered massive opposition protests that were heavily repressed, and which induced the creation of the *Asamblea Nacional Constituyente*, which took over supraconstitutional powers in the hand of the regime. Even if economic events like sanctions, and changing living conditions had no effect on migration outcomes, these strictly political factors could plausibly explain the observed political gradient in migration.

Moreover, it is the evolution of these political events which "triggered" the imposition of sanctions, and these political events could have their own effects of the economy, along with those of other concurrent events within the same year (i.e. sanctions), the military takeover of the oil sector, among others. Moreover, as migration choices are often planned months ahead, it is perfectly possible that the flows observed in 2017 were the result of choices induced by pre-sanctions economic erosion, which accounts for the bulk of the collapse of the Venezuelan economy. It is expected for regime opponents to choose to "exit" in response to the same degree of economic duress (Hirschman, 1970), but even if the results in Idrobo (2024) were driven by the worsening economic conditions and not by the targeted political discrimination and repression that they were being subjected to, claiming that the outmigration of opponents beginning in 2017 is a causal effect of sanctions relies on the implausible assumption that the prior economic trends had no effect on post-2017 migration, and that consequential concurrent events had no economic impacts.

That opponents may have chosen to leave as a response to the same pre-sanctions economic shock or to the economic effects of consequential concurrent events is compounded by the possibility of favoritism in the policy responses to said shocks and events. For instance, if Maduro's response to the economic crisis was to discriminate in favor of its supporters and against opponents (Morales-Arilla, 2022; Morales-Arilla and Abbott, 2024; Morales-Arilla and Traettino, 2024), then the pre-sanctions macroeconomic collapse might have had a disproportionately harsh effect on the living standards of regime opponents. This adds the possibility of favoritism to the set of potential explanations for opponent migration that are not related to sanctions.

The assumptions that Idrobo (2024) needs to make to conclude that his findings are a consequence of the 2017 sanctions are not only implausible, but also untestable, given the low (yearly) frequency in his data. It is especially hard to interpret the 2017 increases in outmigration in opposition-leaning areas as a result of sanctions because the data does not allow us to observe migration choices in the narrow window between sanctions and other consequential treatments. This concern is also relevant for Zambrano et al. (2021), who try to estimate effects of the 2017 sanctions on oil production and essential imports by performing a regression discontinuity specification on monthly data. In our view, the most interesting result of that article is not to show a discontinuous increase in imports at the time that sanctions were first enacted, but to show that the import collapse that the country was experiencing stopped with the 2017 financial sanctions.

Finally, as discussed in Bahar et al. (2019), there are no reasons to expect for *financial* sanctions to trigger immediate effects on oil production or other economic outcomes, as financial markets were effectively closed to the government and PDVSA by the time that sanctions were approved. Indeed, Idrobo (2024) claims that "sanctions and general economic decay effectively exported a significant part of the political opposition," and that the Venezuelan refugee wave "was partly a consequence of the economic sanctions." Unfortunately, the paper does not separate the specific effects of sanctions from those of the "general economic decay" - the majority of which preceded sanctions - from the concurrent harassment of the political opposition, from the potential favoritism in regime responses to the economic crisis, and from the economic effects of consequential concurrent shocks to the economy. Without adequately addressing these, we cannot reject the null hypothesis that the part of the effect that is determined specifically by sanctions is zero without relying on implausible assumptions.

In sum, there are three key critiques on the empirical literature arguing that sanctions worked as a "collective punishment" on Venezuelans. First, the literature fails to identify negative causal effects on imports and on development outcomes. Second, the literature does not separately identify the effects of sanctions from worsening pre-sanctions economic trends. Finally, the literature does not identify the effects of sanctions from those of meaningful concurrent treatments. Having failed to overcome these critiques, we believe the claim that sanctions eroded Venezuelans' living standards is not warranted by the causal quantitative literature. In the following four sections, we introduce original evidence warranting further skepticism on that view.

## 4 Case Study 1: Did the 2017 Financial Sanctions Affect Local Economic Outcomes in Oil-Producing Areas?

The Venezuelan economy is heavily dependent on its oil sector (Organization of the Petroleum Exporting Countries (OPEC), 2024; World Bank, 2025), which has long been centrally controlled by the country's government -mainly through PDVSA, Venezuela's National Oil Company. For this reason, it could be expected that constraints imposed on PDVSA by the 2017 financial sanctions could have had massive effects on the country's economy. At the same time, as discussed earlier, Bahar et al. (2019) show that financial markets were essentially already closed to new debt issuance by PDVSA, making access to fresh financing limited under the no-sanctions counterfactual. Given these contradicting expectations, and since the bulk of the literature discussed earlier has focused on how sanctions affected the Venezuelan economy starting in 2017, how can we assess if the 2017 financial sanctions affected the Venezuelan economy?

The causal chain for sanctions as collective punishment suggests that, beginning in August 2017, they eroded the Venezuelan economy by restricting access to oil export revenues, with the resulting foreign-exchange shortage triggering a collapse in imports of essential goods. This is indeed a "macroeconomic" argument that should affect the economy as a whole. However, different from the 2019 oil sanctions, the 2017 financial sanctions did not affect PDVSA's capacity to market Venezuelan oil in the United States or elsewhere. That is, *if* the 2017 financial sanctions affected oil export revenues, it is not due to their effect on PDVSA's export prices, but because of a reduction in the amount of oil it was able to produce. The 2017 financial sanctions could produce that effect if the oil sector became unable to sustain its working capital and engage in the necessary investments for maintaining its infrastructure and productive capabilities.

If this was indeed happening, the resulting macroeconomic effect should be accompanied by a disproportionate erosion of local economic outcomes in oil-producing areas of the country, as it is their main local economic activity that could be affected by sanction-induced financial constraints on PDVSA. Certainly, observing such an outcome could also be driven by the concurrent institutional and operational treatments experienced in Venezuela during the second half of 2017. However, as all these treatments should in principle affect the oil sector negatively, it would be harder to argue that the 2017 financial sanctions were especially corrosive if economic outcomes in oil-producing areas collapsed at the same rate as those of non-oil-producing areas.

In this case study, we explore whether there was a relative decline in local economic outcomes (nighttime lights, cornflour sales, and local emigration) in oil-producing regions of the country following the 2017 financial sanctions. We leverage municipality-month data on nighttime lights and cornflour sales, as well as municipality-election data on local electoral turnout as a proxy for local migration.[16] Nighttime lights data come from NASA's Visible Infrared Imaging Radiometer Suite (VIIRS), which is aggregated from the grid level to the municipality level to produce a measure of total radiance for each month between 2015 and 2018. We also remove observations affected by gas flaring, in order to avoid outliers that confound the relationship between economic activity nighttime radiance. Monthly proprietary data on cornflour sales by municipality during the same period come from a large food producer within Venezuela. Lastly, municipality turnout data for the 2012, 2013, 2015, and 2018 elections come from Venezuela's *Consejo Nacional Electoral* (CNE), and turnout data for the 2024 elections comes from the ComandoConVenezuela's website.[17]

We begin by examining the trends for per capita nightlights. Figure 4 shows that average values followed a downward trend for both groups before sanctions were first enacted - with the negative trend being somewhat more pronounced in oil-producing regions. Upon sanctions, there was an initial recovery and later deterioration in per capita nighttime lights in both groups, with oil and non-oil municipalities moving in tandem.

[16] Different studies consider local electoral turnout as a proxy for local emigration. Migrants were disenfranchised through limited opportunities to register for voting abroad, and returning to their hometowns to cast their votes can be prohibitively costly. See Morales-Arilla et al. (2025).

[17] The credibility of this data, which was published by the opposition's campaign, has been assessed and validated by several independent analyses. See Corrales and Kronick (2025).

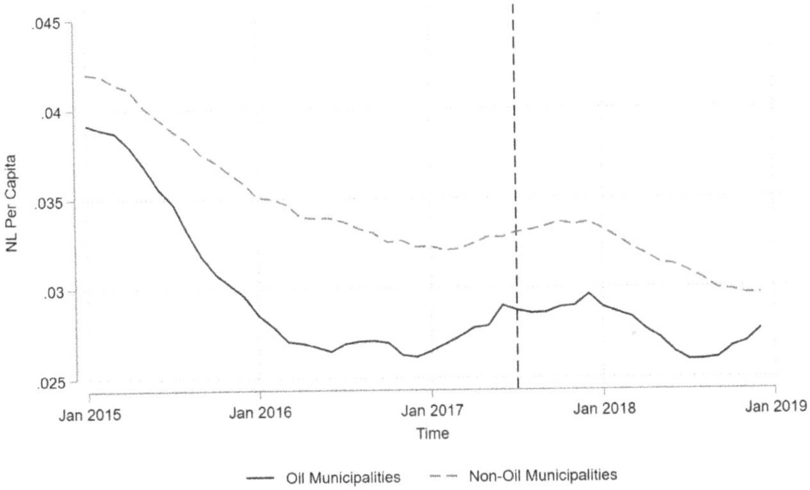


**Figure 4** Intensity of nightlights by municipality type

**Note:** Monthly per capita nighttime light intensity (nW/(cm$^2$·sr)) for oil-producing and non-oil-producing municipalities from January 2015 to December 2018. The vertical dashed line indicates July 2017, the month preceding the imposition of US financial sanctions.

**Source:** NASA's Visible Infrared Imaging Radiometer Suite (VIIRS). Authors' calculations.

Figure 5 focuses on per capita cornflour sales. Same as earlier, average values in both oil-producing and non-oil-producing municipalities experienced a downward trend before sanctions were first enacted. After the 2017 financial sanctions, there is an initial moderate recovery and later collapse in both groups.

Lastly, Figure 6 shows electoral turnout rates in the different national elections between 2012 and 2024. Had the sanctions prompted people to migrate disproportionately from oil areas, we should observe a decrease in their relative turnout rates. However, while average turnout rates dropped for the 2018 and 2024 election in both groups, average turnout levels and their changes after the 2017 financial sanctions are very similar between oil and non-oil municipalities.[18]

We perform a set of difference-in-differences regression specifications to assess whether changes in these outcomes for oil and non-oil municipalities were statistically different from each other. What this approach does is to estimate whether the changes in the "gaps" between these two groups of

[18] The drop in electoral turnout after 2015 was more pronounced for the 2018 presidential elections because of the opposition's boycott. All our later results regarding electoral turnout are robust to removing the 2018 election or the 2024 election, which occurred after the 2019 sanctions and several other relevant treatments.

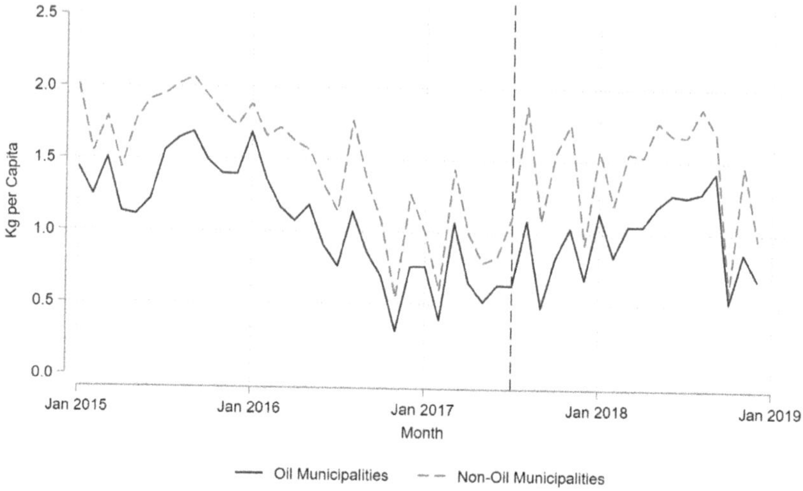


**Figure 5** Evolution of cornflour sales by municipality type

**Note:** Monthly per capita cornflour sales in kilograms for oil-producing and non-oil-producing municipalities from January 2015 to December 2018. The vertical dashed line indicates July 2017, the month preceding the imposition of US financial sanctions.

**Source:** Proprietary data from a large food producer in Venezuela. Authors' calculations.

municipalities after the enactment of financial sanctions in 2017 are sufficiently large so as to consider them significant. The estimates for the effects are found in Table 3. Across all the outcomes of interest, the changes observed in oil municipalities are statistically indistinguishable from those observed in non-oil municipalities. We exclude municipalities that consist of Caracas, the capital of Venezuela. This is due to the special treatment Caracas receives as being the seat of power of the country.[19] Conclusions are unaffected after controlling for baseline local poverty, population density and regime support levels. Similarly, conclusions are also consistent when Caracas is included in the sample. Our robustness checks in Appendix A.2 provide these estimates. This suggests that economic outcomes in oil-producing areas eroded at a similar rate as outcomes in non-oil-producing areas after the 2017 financial sanctions - which is inconsistent with the view that these sanctions limited PDVSA's financing to the point of massively eroding operations in the oil sector.

We complement our difference-in-differences analysis with "Event-Study" analyses, comparing period-specific gaps between oil and non-oil municipalities

[19] In (Morales-Arilla, 2022), there is evidence that Caracas was spared from power rationing following the 2019 blackouts.

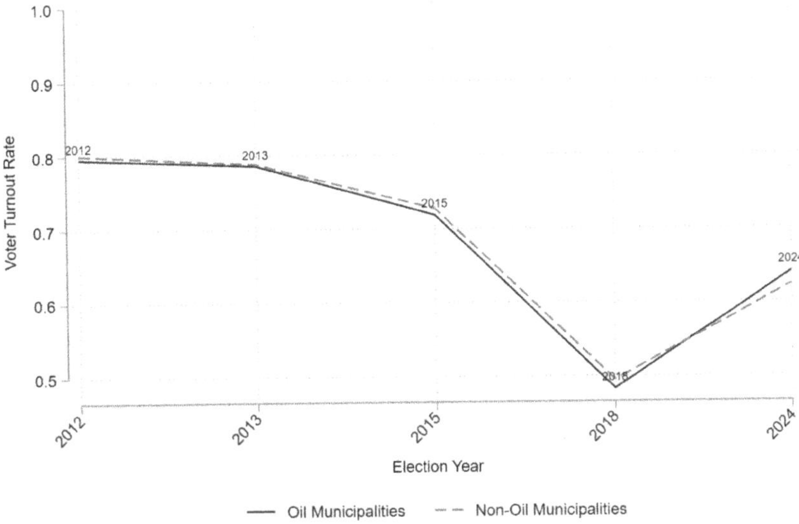


**Figure 6** Voter turnout rates by municipality type

**Note:** Average voter turnout rates (percentage of registered voters who cast ballots) by election year for oil-producing and non-oil-producing municipalities. Data cover presidential elections (2012, 2013, 2018, 2024) and National Assembly elections (2015).

**Sources:** Venezuela's Consejo Nacional Electoral (CNE) for 2012-2018 elections; ComandoConVenezuela for 2024 election. Authors' calculations.

with the gap in the last pre-sanction period in each dataset. By doing so, we can observe whether differences between both groups were constant before sanctions were first enacted -a test for the plausibility of the identifying assumptions in difference-in-differences analyses- along with the timing of the potential effects of sanctions. The black lines in Figure 7 and Figure 8 represent the oil vs. non-oil gap between a specific period and the last period before sanctions, while grey dotted lines indicate the limits of a confidence interval that captures the value of 0 if gap differences are not statistically significant. The reference period for per capita nighttime lights (Figure 7) and cornflour sales (Figure 8) is July 2017, the month right before financial sanctions were first imposed. The reference period for electoral turnout is the 2015 election, the last national election with opposition participation before the enactment of financial sanctions.

Figure 7 shows how differences in per capita nighttime lights between oil and non-oil municipalities were not changing systematically before the enactment of financial sanctions. Most importantly, it also shows how these differences continued largely unchanged upon the enactment of sanctions. Figure 8 shows

**Table 3** Impact of sanctions on outcomes

| | (1) | (2) | (3) | (4) | (5) | (6) |
|---|---|---|---|---|---|---|
| **VARIABLES** | **Per Capita Nightlights ($nW/(cm^2$-$sr)$)** | | **Per Capita Cornflour Sales (Kg)** | | **Electoral Turnout (%)** | |
| Diff-In-Diff Term | −0.0012 | −0.0005 | −0.0495 | −0.0125 | −0.0073 | −0.0178 |
| | (0.0023) | (0.0023) | (0.1079) | (0.0944) | (0.0217) | (0.0217) |
| Observations | 12,408 | 12,408 | 14,880 | 14,880 | 1,448 | 1,448 |
| Adjusted R-squared | 0.969 | 0.969 | 0.546 | 0.549 | 0.868 | 0.927 |
| Municipality FE | Yes | Yes | Yes | Yes | Yes | Yes |
| Month FE | Yes | Yes | Yes | Yes | | |
| Election FE | | | | | Yes | Yes |
| Other Control Variables | No | Yes | No | Yes | No | Yes |

**Note:** Difference-in-differences estimates based on Equation 1 comparing oil-producing versus non-oil-producing municipalities before and after the August 2017 financial sanctions. The dependent variables are per capita nighttime light intensity (columns 1 and 2), per capita cornflour sales in kilograms (columns 3 and 4), and electoral turnout rates as a percentage of registered voters (columns 5 and 6). The difference-in-differences term is the interaction between a post-July 2017 indicator and an oil municipality indicator. Even-numbered columns include controls for baseline population density, poverty rate, and regime support (2013 chavista vote share). Standard errors clustered at the municipality level in parentheses. Caracas is excluded from the sample. Significance levels: *** $p<0.01$, ** $p<0.05$, * $p<0.1$.

**Sources:** VIIRS for nighttime lights; proprietary data for cornflour sales; CNE and ComandoConVenezuela for electoral data. Authors' calculations.

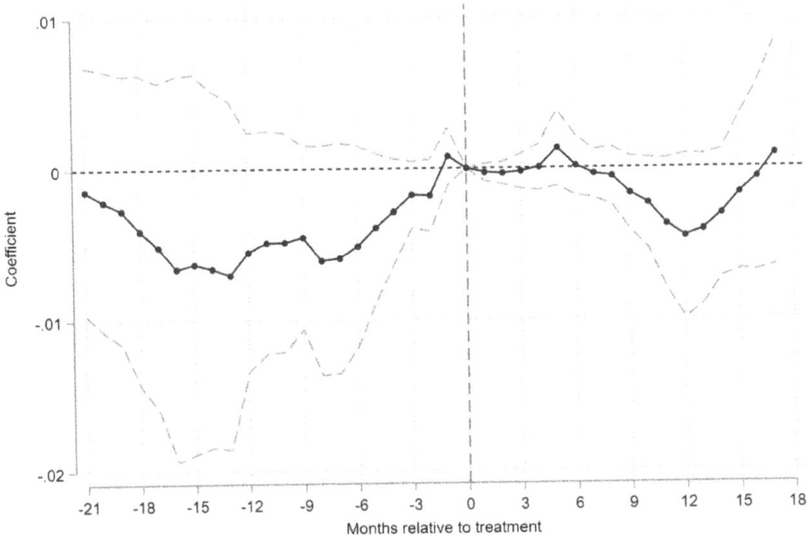


**Figure 7** Event study: Per capita nightlights

**Note:** Event study coefficients based on Equation 2 showing the difference in per capita nighttime light intensity between oil-producing and non-oil-producing municipalities relative to July 2017 (month 0). Each point represents the interaction coefficient between month indicators and the oil municipality indicator. The regression includes municipality and month fixed effects, as well as controls for baseline population density, poverty rate, and regime support. Dashed lines indicate 95% confidence intervals. Standard errors are clustered at the municipality level.

**Source:** NASA's Visible Infrared Imaging Radiometer Suite (VIIRS). Authors' calculations.

similar patterns before and after sanctions for the gap in per capita sales of cornflour between oil and non-oil municipalities. Lastly, Figure 9 confirms similar patterns for electoral turnout.

Overall, our event-study analyses confirm the validity and the conclusions of our earlier difference-in-differences analyses. We find no statistically significant changes in the differences between oil and non-oil municipalities after the enactment of financial sanctions in August 2017. As discussed earlier, a relative worsening of outcomes in oil-producing areas was to be expected if financial sanctions had an effect on oil production, which was the main mechanism through which they could have affected the country's oil revenues. These results cast further doubt on the view that financial sanctions were a consequential cause behind Venezuela's economic collapse. We provide further details regarding the data and empirical strategies in the A.2 Technical Appendix for Case Study 1.

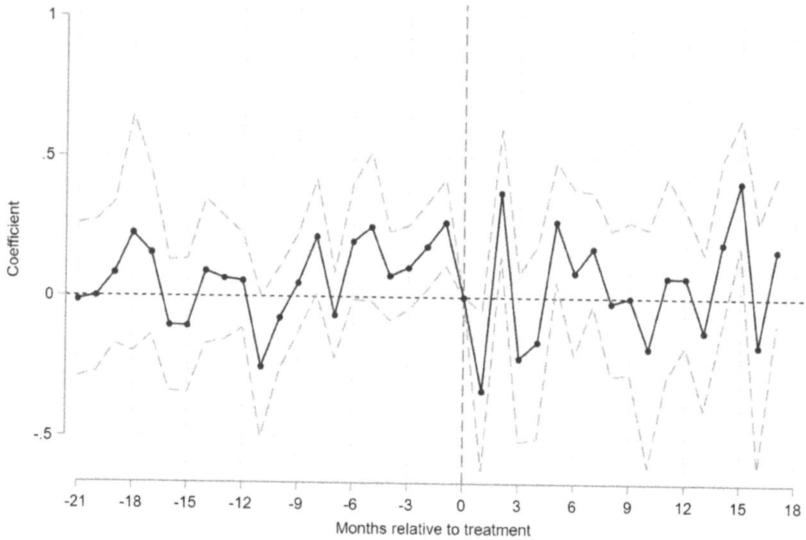


**Figure 8** Event study: Cornflour sales

**Note:** Event study coefficients based on Equation 2 showing the difference in per capita cornflour sales (kilograms) between oil-producing and non-oil-producing municipalities relative to July 2017 (month 0). Each point represents the interaction coefficient between month indicators and the oil municipality indicator. The regression includes municipality and month fixed effects, as well as controls for baseline population density, poverty rate, and regime support. Dashed lines indicate 95% confidence intervals. Standard errors are clustered at the municipality level.

**Source:** Proprietary data from a large food producer in Venezuela. Authors' calculations.

## 5 Case Study 2: Parsing Concurrent Treatments through the Effects of the 2019 Blackouts

In the context of sanctions, which are often triggered or followed by consequential events, identifying treatment-specific effects requires that we take advantage of the short time gaps between each other. Suppose we care about the effect of treatment $B$, which was shortly preceded by treatment $A$ and shortly followed by treatment $C$, on outcome $Y$. To adequately estimate the effect of $B$, we need for three conditions to be met:

1. **Treatments should not "trigger"[20] each other:** While events are happening in short proximity to each other in this environment, they should occur at *some* distance from each other. This is key for observing variation in

[20] By "trigger" we mean for one event to immediately induce the occurrence of other.

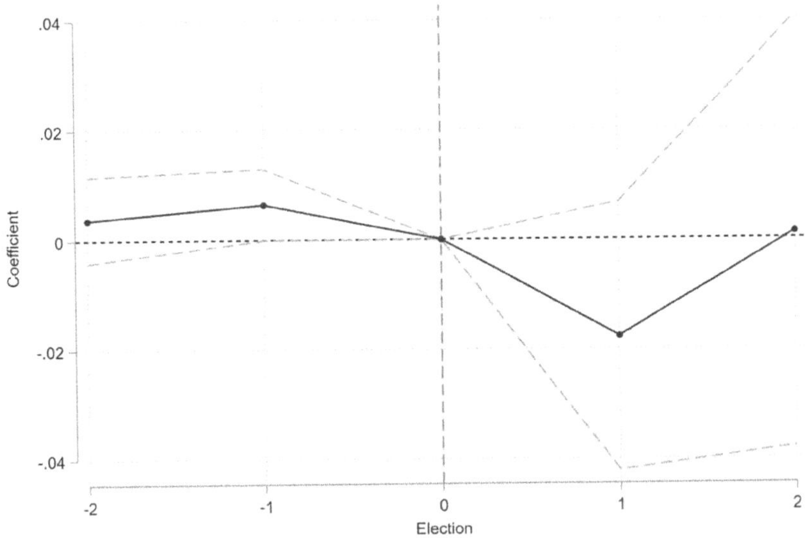


**Figure 9** Event study: Voter turnout rates

**Note:** Event study coefficients based on Equation 2 showing the difference in voter turnout rates (percentage of registered voters) between oil-producing and non-oil-producing municipalities relative to the 2015 election (election 0). Each point represents the interaction coefficient between election year indicators and the oil municipality indicator. The regression includes municipality and election fixed effects, as well as controls for baseline population density, poverty rate, and regime support. Dashed lines indicate 95% confidence intervals. Standard errors are clustered at the municipality level.

**Sources:** Venezuela's Consejo Nacional Electoral (CNE) for 2012–2018 elections; ComandoConVenezuela for 2024 election. Authors' calculations.

*Y* at the time that *B* occurs that cannot be explained by the immediate effects of other treatments.

2. **Treatment *B* must have immediate effects on *Y*:** As *B* is shortly preceded by *A*, effects of *A* may already be kicking in by the time that *B* occurs. If the effects of *A* are dynamic, it will be hard to differentiate the independent effects of *A* and *B* in the variation of *Y* after *B* occurs without relying in implausible assumptions. However, if the nature of *B* is that it should have an immediate, discrete effect on outcome *Y*, we could then estimate the effect of *B* by looking at the discontinuous change in outcome *Y* at the time that *B* occurs. Interpreting this change in *Y* as the causal effect of *B* relies on the continuity assumption that the effect of *A* is about the same right before and right after *B* occurs, a typical assumption in temporal regression discontinuity designs (tRDD). Such designs would be plausible if *B* is not triggered by *A*, *C* is not triggered by *B*, and there are theoretical reasons to think that *B* has an immediate effect on outcome *Y*.

3. **Data with very high periodicity is available:** The need for *B* to have immediate effects is also because we need to observe its effects before *C* occurs, as changes in *Y* that occur afterward would confound the effects of all three treatments. Because all three treatments are occurring in very short proximity to each other, any estimation exercise would require for us to observe substantial variation in *Y* within the narrow time frames separating *B* from *A* and *B* from *C*. Hence, estimating the size of the immediate effect of *B* requires high periodicity data on *Y*.

We believe that none of these conditions are met for the study of sanctions on Venezuela because of the following reasons:

- **Sanctions were triggered by relevant events with independent effects:** The 2017 financial sanctions were triggered by the creation of the *ANC*, which essentially usurped all legislative prerogatives and assumed supra-constitutional power in the hands of the regime. The 2019 oil sanctions were triggered by the start of the constitutional crisis, which also triggered a massive wave of protests and the change in international recognition of who the de jure president of the country really was. From the perspective of our discussion earlier, the fact that sanctions were triggered means that it is extremely hard to estimate independent effects adequately without relying on the implausible assumption that the triggering factors would not have had a negative effect on economic outcomes had sanctions not been implemented.
- **Sanctions should not have immediate effects on economic outcomes:** The 2017 financial sanctions did not restrict commercial relations with Venezuela, but only constrained the Venezuelan Government and PDVSA from accessing United States' financial markets, access which was de facto already closed because of the country's and PDVSA's insolvency (Bahar et al., 2019). If relevant, financial sanctions could only reduce exports by disrupting operations in the oil sector, something that would not happen immediately, as working capital requirements for services and maintenance would need to accumulate to the point that bond emissions for fresh financing would become necessary (but impossible due to sanctions). Similarly, the 2019 oil sanctions were designed with months-long lags to allow foreign firms to wind down their activities.
- **Publicly available data on economic outcomes is of low frequency given the narrow periods between concurrent treatments:** The vast majority of the literature on this question focuses on available sources of oil exports and imports of essential goods at yearly or monthly frequency. In this environment of multiple concurrent treatments, such periodicity is inadequately low to study the causal effects of interest. For instance, there were only three

months between the 2017 financial sanctions and the military takeover of operations in Venezuela's oil sector. Similarly, there was only a month and a half between the 2019 oil sanctions and the nationwide blackouts of early March that same year.

We believe this criticism is relevant for essentially all contributions in the literature on the effects of economic sanctions on oil production and developmental outcomes in Venezuela. While this is true for sanctions, we believe it is not necessarily true for all concurrent treatments. In this section, we focus on the blackouts of March 7, 2019. We pay attention to the blackouts for two reasons. First, blackouts occurred shortly after the 2019 oil sanctions. If we are able to adequately identify causal effects of the blackouts on key outcomes of interest in the causal chain associated with sanctions, this would confirm the confounding of a multiplicity of treatments in arguing that post-sanctions economic events can be attributed as the causal effect of sanctions. Second, from the perspective of the criteria outlined earlier, the blackouts are a good candidate for identification of causal effects in the context of multiple concurrent treatments.

First, blackouts were not triggered by any of the other concurrent events. Indeed, while the start of the constitutional crisis and the oil sanctions occurred on January 23, 2019, these events did not have any direct effect on power generation and transmission. Blackouts occurred weeks later, triggered by an unrelated disruption in the power transmission system.[21] Second, beyond the obvious abrupt effects that blackouts can have on key economic and social outcomes, there are technological reasons to believe that the effects of power supply disruptions on oil production should be immediate. This is because most of the oil production in Venezuela relies on the injection of steam to pump oil out of active wells. This process of injection is energy intensive and relies on access to the country's power grid. Finally, while not public, there are daily and oil-field specific production data collected by consulting firms analyzing Venezuela's oil sector.[22] For these reasons, estimating blackout-specific causal effects through daily production drops on the day of the blackouts would be possible under the plausible assumption that the effects of prior treatments, such as the constitutional crisis and sanctions, do not change discretely at the onset of the blackouts.

A first look at daily aggregates of oil production in Venezuela already conveys the immediate and large importance of blackouts with regard to other

21 More details on the specifics of the 2019 blackouts are provided in Morales Arilla (2022).

22 The analyses presented next are based on daily, oil-field-specific data from one such firm which shall remain anonymous.

factors in explaining events in the oil sector during 2019. Panel A of Figure 10 shows a mild downward trend the days before March 7, 2019, after which there was an immediate and massive collapse in oil output that cannot be understood through explanations other than the blackouts. Afterward, oil production did not recover to pre-blackout levels and became much more sclerotic, as aftershocks in power supply continued to plague the country for long after the initial blackout. As mentioned, the main connection between power supply accessibility and oil production in Venezuela is technological in nature, as oil fields accounting for most of the production rely on steam injection ("Pump" fields), which is an energy intensive process in itself. Fields accounting for a minority of production rely on associated natural gas for pushing oil out of the well ("Gas" fields). Indeed, Panel B of Figure 10 provides a production index separating events in the oil sector between "Pump" and "Gas" fields. While both kinds of fields were affected by the blackouts, we can observe how blackouts affect "Pump" fields disproportionately.

We formalize this analysis to estimate the average effect of the 2019 blackout on the production of Venezuelan oil fields through a regression-discontinuity specification.[23] Panel A of Figure 11 shows average production indices on different days two weeks before and after the blackouts. The blackout led to a drop of 28 percentage points in the production of the average oil field. Decisively, as shown in Panel B of Figure 11, this effect was much stronger on "Pump" dependent fields: While Blackout-induced production drops in the average "Gas" field were of 14 percentage points, the average loss in "Pump" fields was of 42 percentage points.

Given the relative production magnitudes of different fields within the country, we perform regression-discontinuity estimations for each separate field. Our results, portrayed in Figure 12, confirm that the distribution of effects is significantly more negative for "Pump" fields, and shows that some of these fields suffered blackout-induced losses of over 75 percentage points. With these estimates and the baseline productivity of each field, we can estimate that the country lost 728,000 daily barrels of oil - about 50% of its daily productivity in early January 2019 - as an immediate consequence of the blackouts.

By design, these effects are estimated in the immediate aftermath of the nationwide blackouts of March 7, which lasted for almost a full week. The disruptions to oil production driven by the blackouts may have had a lasting influence on events in the oil sector. For instance, a large portion of the oil production in the country is concentrated in the Orinoco belt, which produces

[23] Additional methodological details are provided in the Appendix.

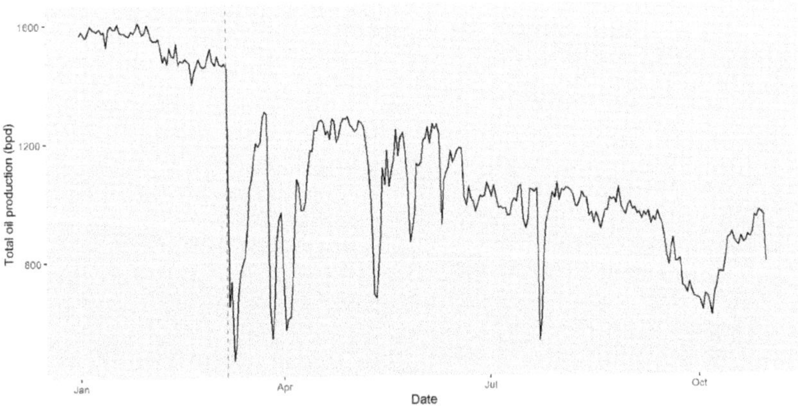


(a) Daily oil production (bpd)

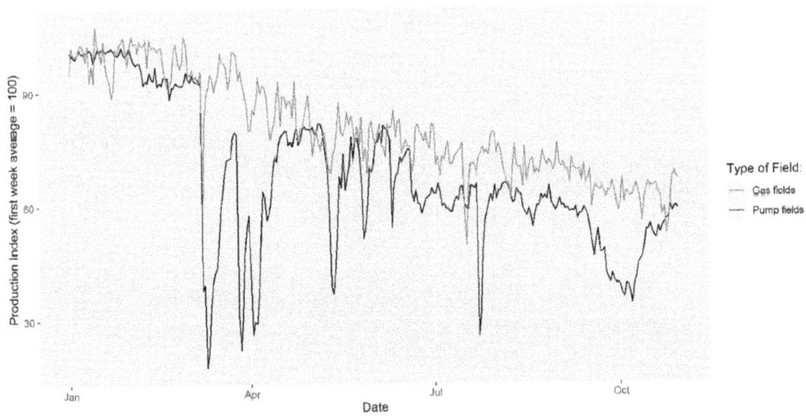


(b) Indexed Differences

**Figure 10** Daily oil production by field type

**Note:** Panel A shows total daily oil production in barrels per day (bpd) from January to October 2019. Panel B shows production indices (first week of January 2019 = 100) separately for "Pump" fields (requiring steam injection) and "Gas" fields (relying on associated natural gas). The vertical line marks March 7, 2019, when nationwide electrical blackouts began.

**Source:** Proprietary daily field-level production data from an oil consulting firm. Authors' calculations.

extra-heavy oils. Production in this region is hard to restart, as such extra-heavy oils can solidify and clog pipelines if they stop flowing. Perhaps most importantly, the disruption that triggered the original blackout that year had a sustained effect on power supply in the country. Shorter nationwide blackouts occurred as aftershocks in the following weeks, and power supply became generally very unreliable.

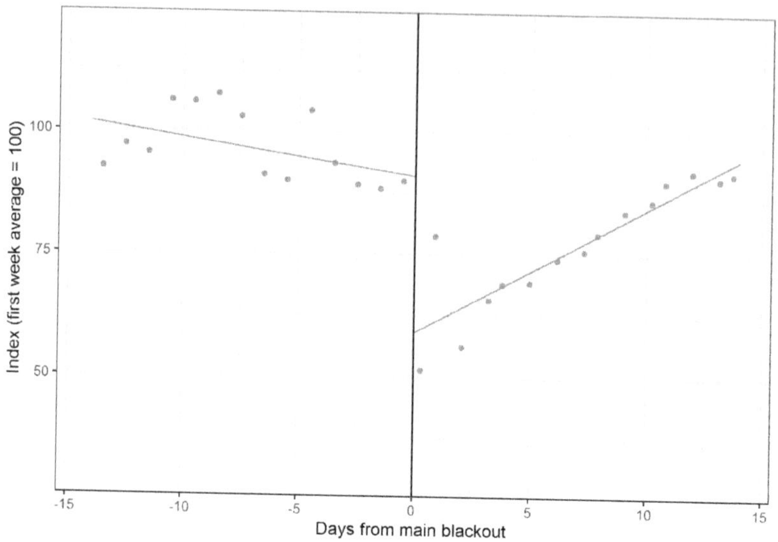


(a) Effect on the average field

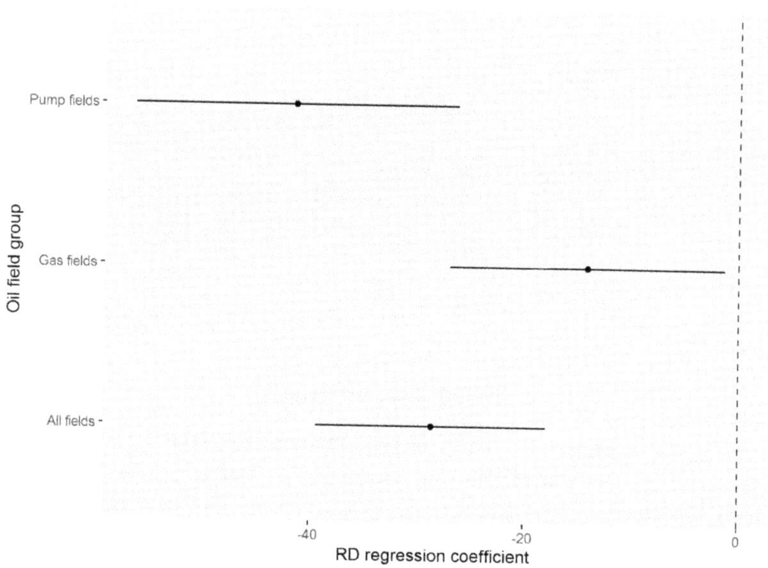


(b) Average effect by field type

**Figure 11** Immediate effect of power blackouts by field type

**Note:** Panel A shows regression discontinuity estimates of the blackout effect on oil production indices following Equation 3. Points represent average daily production indices across all fields, with fitted lines showing predicted values two weeks before and after March 7, 2019. Panel B presents coefficient estimates and 95% confidence intervals from separate regression discontinuity specifications for "Pump" fields (steam injection) and "Gas" fields (natural gas) and the full set of oil fields. A bandwidth of two weeks was determined following the Calonico et al. (2020) optimal bandwidth selection procedure. Standard errors are clustered at the field level.

**Source:** Proprietary daily field-level production data from an oil consulting firm. Authors' calculations.

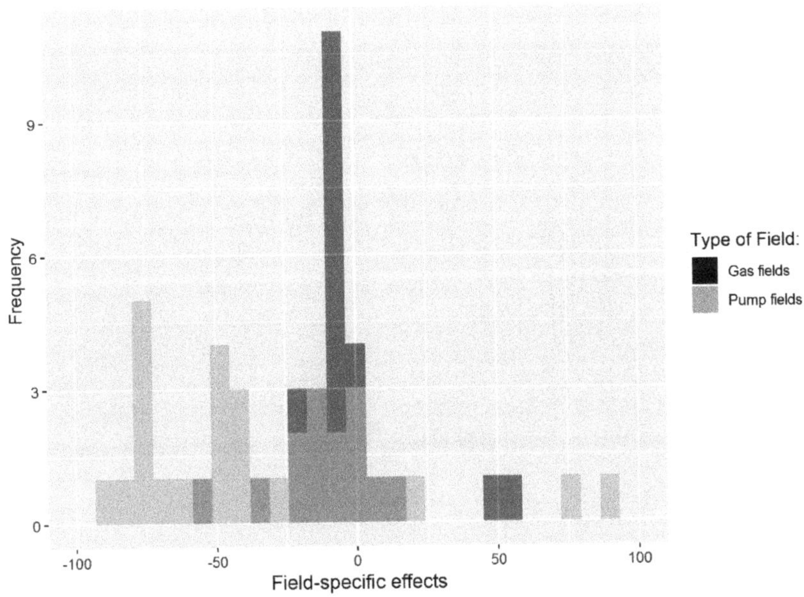


**Figure 12** Distribution of field-specific effects

**Note:** Overlapping histograms showing the distribution of field-specific regression discontinuity estimates of the March 7, 2019, blackout effect on oil production. Each estimate represents the percentage point change in production index for an individual oil field. "Pump" fields require steam injection for extraction; "Gas" fields rely on associated natural gas. Estimates are from separate regression discontinuity specifications for each of the sixty-four oil fields in the dataset, using a two-week bandwidth.

**Source:** Proprietary daily field-level production data from an oil consulting firm. Authors' calculations.

However lasting the effects of the blackouts, they start to confound with the potential effects of other concurrent events during periods further into the future. Nevertheless, we can still use the relative underperformance of "Pump" fields versus "Gas" fields after the original blackouts and consider daily international oil price values to estimate a "lowest possible" aggregate effect of blackouts. This exercise, which builds no-blackout counterfactuals for "Pump" fields based on the evolution of production in "Gas" fields, relies on the implausible assumption that power-supply disruptions had no effect on the latter - something which our prior analysis rules out. Panels A and B of Figure 13 show daily and cumulative production losses in dollar value in total and the amount explained by the relative underperformance of "Pump" fields relative to "Gas" fields after the blackout of March 7. According to this analysis, the lowest possible effect of blackouts on oil production values between March 7 and October 31, 2019 was $2.3 billion, or 33% of the losses incurred during

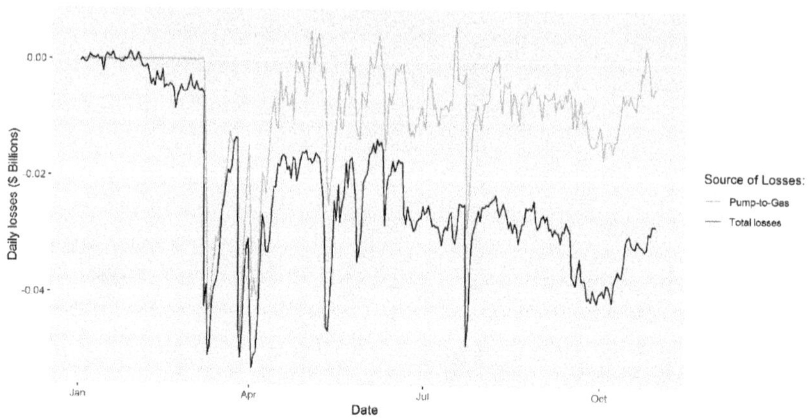


(a) Daily

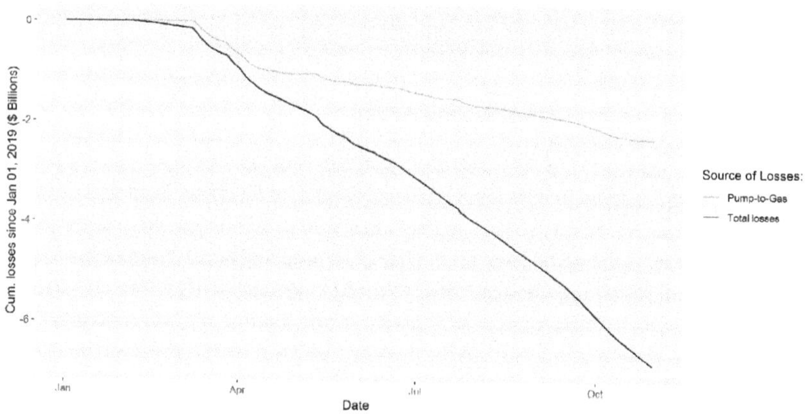


(b) Cumulative

**Figure 13** Lowest-possible blackout-induced production losses

**Note:** Panel A shows daily oil production losses in million USD calculated using WTI oil prices. Total losses (black line) represent the difference between actual production and early January 2019 baseline levels. Losses attributed to relative underperformance of "Pump" fields versus "Gas" fields (light gray line) are calculated assuming "Gas" fields were unaffected by power disruptions. Panel B shows cumulative losses from January 1 to October 31, 2019.

**Source:** Proprietary daily field-level production data from an oil consulting firm; WTI oil prices from commodity markets. Authors' calculations.

that period. We provide further details about this calculation and about our data and regression discontinuity analyses in the Technical appendix for Case Study 2.

Our goal in focusing on the blackouts of 2019 in this section was twofold. First, we show how circumstances specific to the blackout (not triggered by other relevant events, immediate effects and high-periodicity data) allowed us to adequately estimate its causal effects amid concurrent treatments. Unfortunately, the fact that none of these conditions are met in the case of the 2017 financial and 2019 oil sanctions on Venezuela means that the estimates prevalent in the literature are not identifying the specific effects of sanctions in relation to those of consequential concurrent treatments. Perhaps most importantly, by identifying the very large effects of the blackouts on oil production, we show the first-order biases that the current literature is incurring in by considering all post-sanctions deterioration in economic outcomes as a consequence of sanctions.

## 6 Case Study 3: Did Sanctions Affect the Access to Essential Imports?

What happened to essential imports after sanctions were first implemented? As mentioned earlier, debates over the discontinuous increase in imports after the 2017 financial sanctions (Zambrano et al., 2021; Rodríguez, 2022b) did not highlight what we believe was the key message in their analyses: that the pre-sanctions collapsing trend in imports seems to ameliorate after sanctions. Figure 14 captures this point clearly. The black marks yearly Venezuelan food imports in billions of dollars, while the light gray line adds medicine imports to food imports as a measure of "essential" imports. The collapse in the dark line and in the difference between the dark and light gray lines before 2017 suggests that both food and medicine imports collapsed substantially after 2012, and had reached historically low levels before the first sanctions were imposed. Importantly, we see that both lines become flat and parallel after 2017, as the first set of sanctions were enacted.

Beyond describing the evolution of Venezuelan essential imports, can we credibly estimate what they would have been in the absence of sanctions? For the many reasons discussed earlier regarding oil production, we believe that a credible counterfactual cannot be built. Nevertheless, it is valuable to pursue the same methodologies introduced in the analyses of oil production to evaluate whether the conclusions these methodologies deliver regarding essential imports map out to expectations from the "collective punishment" perspective on sanctions. This is key to understand if sanctions were the cause of Venezuela's economic collapse. In this case study, we pursue the synthetic controls methodology introduced for the analysis of oil production by Rodríguez (2019).

The synthetic control methodology (Abadie and Gardeazabal, 2003; Abadie et al., 2010) provides a data-driven technique to propose a "synthetic" counterfactual built as the weighted average of non-treated "donor" units that best

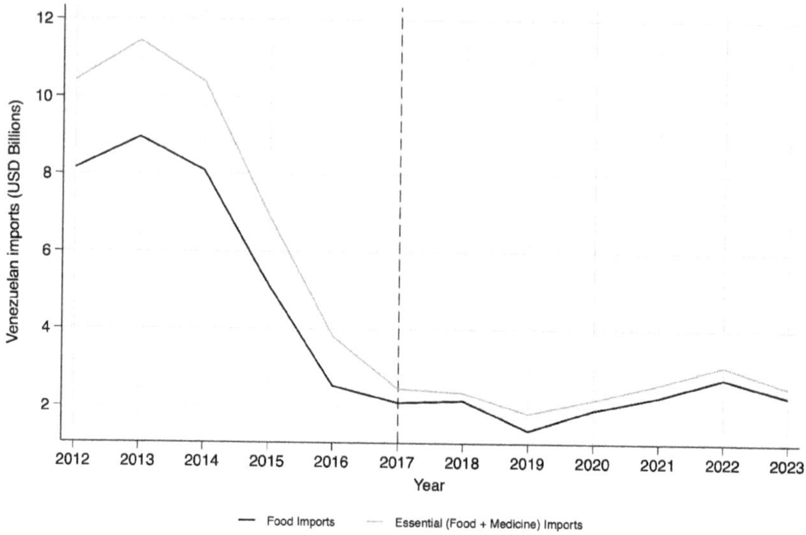


**Figure 14** Evolution of essential imports

**Note:** Annual Venezuelan imports in billions of USD from 2012 to 2023. The black line shows food imports (HS codes < 25, excluding 23, 13, 12, 05, and 0101). The light gray line shows essential imports, combining food and medicine imports (HS code 30). Vertical dashed lines indicate the imposition of US financial sanctions (August 2017).

**Source:** Harvard Growth Lab's Atlas of Economic Complexity. Authors' calculations.

represents the relevant outcome of an uniquely treated unit before the treatment occurred. We perform this technique to capture the evolution of an essential imports index representing essential imports of a given year as a proportion of the essential imports of the same country in 2012. While Zambrano et al. (2021) and Rodríguez (2022b) are able to use monthly Venezuelan imports, such data is not comparably available for the full set of donor countries. For this reason, we look at countries' yearly essential imports. Chiefly, we train the algorithm to fit Venezuela's essential import index between 2012 and 2016, and evaluate effects from 2018 onward.[24]

[24] There is a question on whether to consider 2017 as pre-treatment or post-treatment. The financial sanctions were enacted in August that year, so while most of that year was "pre-treatment," some of the potential effects of sanctions on essential imports could have plausibly materialized in the last quarter of the year. We believe this is not the case because, as was shown by Zambrano et al. (2021) and Rodríguez (2022b), there was no discontinuous drop in Venezuelan essential imports in the months immediately following the enactment of the 2017 financial sanctions. Because of this, while we do not train the synthetic control algorithm to fit on Venezuela's 2017 essential import index in our preferred specification, we do consider 2017 as the last pre-treatment year. Results and conclusions are essentially unchanged if we train the algorithm to also fit on Venezuela's 2017 essential import index.

We filter the pool of potential donor countries by excluding small island nations and territories, and chiefly by excluding all other countries facing economic sanctions or similar treatment from the United States during the period of analysis (Russia, Syria, Cuba, North Korea, Iran, Sudan, Belarus, and Myanmar). The synthetic control methodology chose the following weights: 72.5% Angola, 14.5% Bhutan, 13% Ukraine, 0% all other countries. Figure 15 shows the main results from the analysis, presenting the essential imports of Venezuela and its synthetic counterfactual (Panel A) and the difference between the two (Panel B). While the synthetic Venezuela tracks the evolution of essential imports until 2015, it is unable to capture the collapse of imports observed in 2016 despite being designed to match on that value. Chiefly, while Venezuelan essential imports continued to fall in 2017, the synthetic Venezuela started to recover. In the post-treatment period, changes in the difference between the two are driven by the evolution of the synthetic Venezuela, not by drastic changes in Venezuela's essential import index. In 2017, the difference between the two indices was 44.5 percentage points, while by 2023 the difference was 47.5 percentage points. This means that 94% of the difference in 2023 essential imports between Venezuela and its synthetic counterfactual could be explained by pre-sanctions differences already observed by 2017.

Are these differences statistically significant? In the context of synthetic control exercises, the way to assess whether post-treatment dynamics are too unlikely in the absence of systematic effects is by comparing the difference between the treatment unit and its synthetic counterfactual to the "placebo" differences that would come from replicating the same exercises for the full list of potential donor units. For effects to be significant, post-treatment differences in the treatment unit would have to be disproportionately large in comparison to those of the placebo units. However, Panel A of Figure 16 shows that this is not the case in the context of Venezuela's essential import index, where many of the donor countries show worse post-treatment performances than that of Venezuela. Panel B of Figure 14 shows specific estimates for the probability that each of the post-treatment Venezuelan differences are driven by chance, showing values consistently above 60%. These results indicate that the observed post-treatment decrease in essential imports in Venezuela relative to its synthetic counterfactual is both tiny and statistically insignificant.

It has been argued that synthetic controls allow for substantive "researcher degrees of freedom" which allow for the possibility that analysts tweak specifications to obtain a desired result (Ferman et al., 2020). For this reason, we decided to fit our synthetic control algorithm fitting strictly on pre-treatment values of the outcome variable and not on other arbitrarily chosen variables (Lu, 2021). Moreover, we tried several different specifications along the most

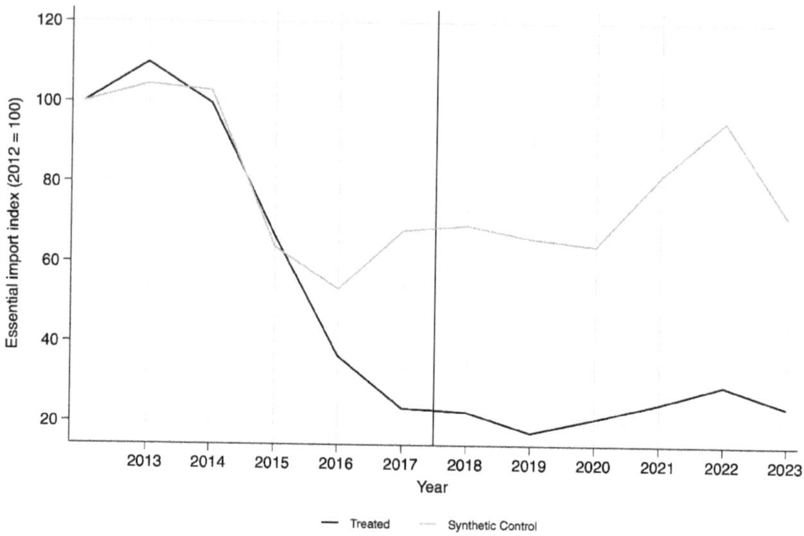


(a) Actual vs. Synthetic

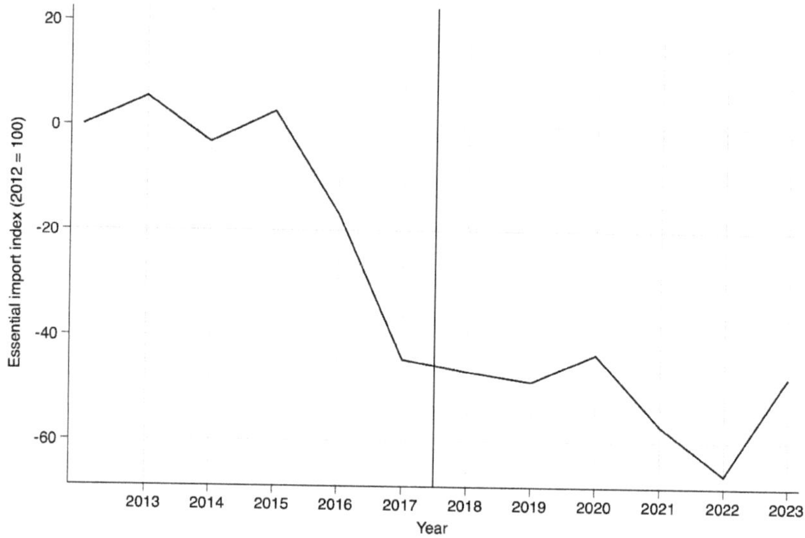


(b) Difference

**Figure 15** Essential import index: Venezuela vs. synthetic counterfactual

**Note:** Panel A shows the essential import index (2012 = 100) for Venezuela and its synthetic control unit from 2013 to 2023. The synthetic control is constructed as a weighted average of non-sanctioned donor countries (72.5% Angola, 14.5% Bhutan, 13% Ukraine) that best matches Venezuela's pre-treatment essential import trends (2012-2016). Panel B shows the difference between actual and synthetic values. Vertical dashed lines indicate US financial sanctions (August 2017).

**Source:** Harvard Growth Lab's Atlas of Economic Complexity. Authors' calculations using synthetic control methodology (Abadie et al., 2010).

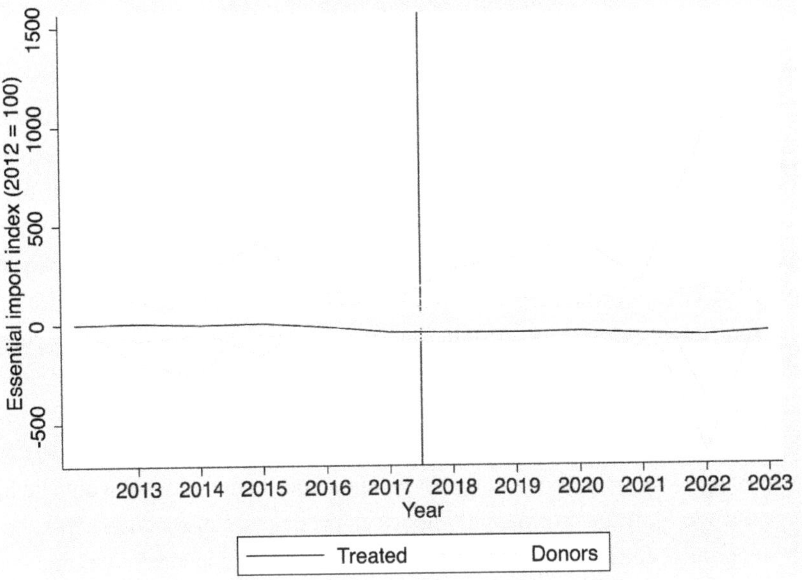


(a) Venezuela vs. placebo differences

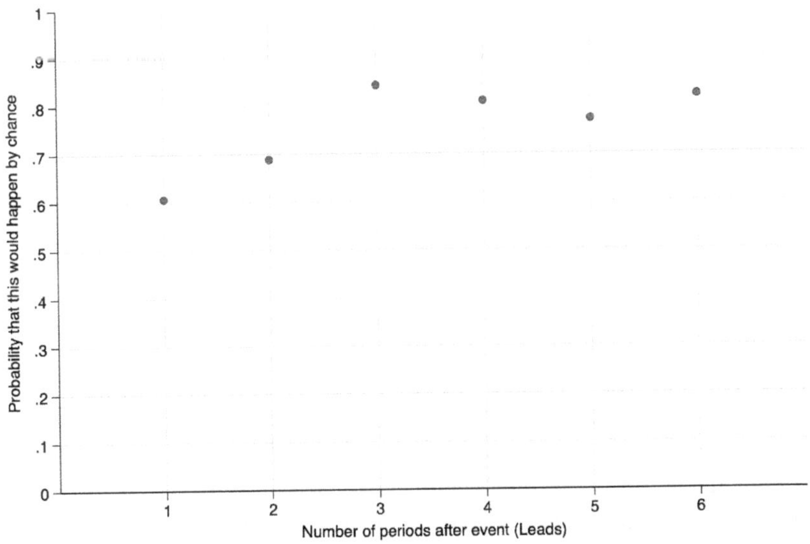


(b) Significance of post-treatment estimates

**Figure 16** Significance of essential import changes after sanctions

**Note:** Panel A shows the difference between actual and synthetic essential import indices for Venezuela (black line) and placebo tests for all potential donor countries (gray lines). Panel B shows p-values for Venezuela's post-treatment differences (2018–2023), calculated as the proportion of placebo units with larger absolute differences than Venezuela in each year. P-values above 0.10 indicate differences are not statistically significant at conventional levels.

**Source:** Harvard Growth Lab's Atlas of Economic Complexity. Authors' calculations using the synthetic control methodology (Abadie et al., 2010).

relevant margins. For example, we replicated this exercise changing our outcome variable to the logarithm of essential imports. We also replicated our exercise limiting the pool of potential donor countries to the same set of countries considered in Rodríguez (2019). Overall, while the quality of pre-treatment matches until 2021 worsens under these alternative specifications, the main conclusion that differences in essential imports between Venezuela and its synthetic counterfactual occur until 2017, and that post-sanctions changes are not statistically significant, remain unchanged. We provide additional details about our synthetic control specifications in the Technical appendix for Case Study 3.

Now again, as highlighted earlier for the case of oil production, we do not believe that this methodology offers a valid counterfactual of what would have happened to Venezuelan essential imports in the absence of sanctions, because this approach does not capture the potential effects of concurrent treatments. However, it is very interesting to show that the synthetic control exercise is unable to track the collapse in imports of 2016 even as it was designed to match on that value. This pre-treatment relative drop is also observed in Rodríguez (2019) but is inadequately attributed to the effects of lower oil prices. Moreover, this exercise shows that pursuing similar methodologies to those used to argue that sanctions led to a decrease in oil production would have revealed a negligible effect on essential imports, highlighting a breakdown in the causal chain behind the argument that sanctions worked as a collective punishment on Venezuelans.

## 7 Case Study 4: Sanctions and the End of Foreign Exchange Controls

Venezuela's foreign exchange control systems created one of the most distortive economic policy frameworks in modern Latin American history. These systems fundamentally warped Venezuela's economy through a complex web of perverse incentives that enriched a small elite while impoverishing the broader population and destroying the country's long-term productive potential. The distortive incentive structure remained in place for over sixteen years, from CADIVI's establishment in 2003 until the final elimination of its successor, DICOM, in May 2019.

### *The Architecture and Consequences of Foreign Exchange Controls*

CADIVI (Commission for the Administration of Foreign Exchange) was established by Presidential Decree No. 2302 on February 5, 2003, designed to prevent capital flight and preserve foreign reserves during a period of political instability following a two-month oil strike (Banco Central de Venezuela, 2003). The system set multiple official exchange rates - typically far below market rates, and required government approval for all foreign currency purchases (Norton Rose Fulbright, 2014). The Bank for International Settlements documented how this created a centralized currency allocation process in which "the Central Bank of Venezuela fixed a monthly allocation of foreign currency to be administered by CADIVI, purchases foreign currency from residents, and sells foreign currency to the public and private sectors subject to approval from CADIVI" (Bank for International Settlements, 2005).

The system created immediate arbitrage opportunities. With official rates often 50–90% below black-market rates, those with access to "official" dollars could generate enormous profits on the spot. The system enabled "$1,000 to be turned into $1 million in a matter of days" (Adam Smith Institute, 2024). This gap between official and parallel rates became the foundation for systematic rent-seeking behavior throughout the economy. The subsidy implicit in cheap official dollars created powerful incentives for importers to manipulate their transactions. Since foreign currency was priced below market rates, "an entire industry of non-productive ghost companies cropped up to lobby the government for subsidized dollars (to resell them on the black market for an immediate profit)" (Economics Observatory, 2024). Early in the process, analysts observed that "many genuine businesses also specialized away from productive activities towards securing cheap dollars" (Fletcher, 2004).

This was carried out through several well-documented mechanisms. According to US State Department investment climate reports, importers would systematically manipulate the system: "Firms often wait 180-270 days to receive dollars, or never receive them, despite having their applications approved," creating powerful incentives for corruption and overpricing (U.S. Department of State, 2015). Court documents from United States' corruption prosecutions reveal that shell companies would issue fraudulent invoices for non-existent or overpriced goods, while transfer pricing manipulation allowed related companies to set artificial prices for intra-company transactions (United States Department of Justice, 2020). The government's limited oversight capacity, combined with the technical complexity of verifying international prices across thousands of products, made this manipulation relatively easy. Import licenses became more valuable than an actual import business, leading to the emergence of what economists called "briefcase importers" who existed solely to capture foreign exchange subsidies.

The discretionary nature of foreign exchange allocation transformed CADIVI and its successors into systematic corruption mechanisms throughout their sixteen-year existence. According to *Transparencia Venezuela*, a prominent anti-corruption organization, President Nicolás Maduro himself admitted the extent of the problem in 2014, creating a presidential commission to investigate how the exchange control system had been breached, with corruption costs estimated at $25 billion by the former Minister of Planning (Transparencia Venezuela, 2021). FinCEN, the United States Treasury's Financial Crimes Enforcement Network, issued a comprehensive advisory in September 2020 documenting the systematic nature of Venezuelan corruption, specifically highlighting how "Venezuelan officials manipulated currency exchange rates and restricted access to U.S. dollars" to extract rents from the economy (Financial Crimes Enforcement Network, 2020). The advisory noted that even when dollars were allocated through official channels, the aforementioned delays created additional opportunities for corruption and favoritism (Financial Crimes Enforcement Network, 2020). Federal court documents from multiple prosecutions reveal the industrial scale of the corruption. Venezuelan officials converted "$40 million in PDVSA funds into approximately $600 million through currency manipulation" (United States Department of Justice, 2020). These prosecutions demonstrate how access to subsidized foreign currency became a form of political patronage distributed to reward loyalty.

The most spectacular example of systematic corruption was the case of Alejandro "El Tuerto" Andrade, Hugo Chávez's bodyguard-later-turned-National Treasurer. Andrade admitted to receiving over $1 billion in bribes from coconspirators in exchange for using his position as Venezuelan national treasurer to select them to conduct currency exchange transactions at favorable rates (United States Department of Justice, 2019). He received cash as well as private jets, yachts, cars, homes, champion horses, and high-end watches from his accomplices (U.S. Department of the Treasury, 2019b). Records show that Andrade accumulated $304 million while squandering opulence in South Florida, but this was just part of a money laundering scheme involving more than $1 billion in bribes (Itempnews Project, 2022). For reference, the construction firm Odebrecht admitted to paying $788 million in bribes across twelve countries in the *Lava Jato* case, the largest corruption scandal in Latin American history and "largest foreign bribery case in history" (United States Department of Justice, 2016).

Beyond corruption, the scandal at the *Productora y Distribuidora Venezolana de Alimentos* (PDVAL), also known as the *Pudreval* scandal, exemplifies how these incentives generated massive waste in food imports. The scandal involved "the finding of tons of rotten food supplies in mid 2010 imported during Hugo Chávez's government through subsidies of state-owned enterprise PDVAL" (Valery, 2010). Venezuelan authorities documented that between 130,000 and 170,000 tons of food supplies were affected, with the political opposition calculating this could have fed 17 million Venezuelans for a month (Agencia EFE, 2010). The fact that PDVAL imported more food than it was able to distribute was not incompetence but rational behavior under the incentive structure created by the exchange controls. State companies faced soft budget constraints as losses were covered by oil revenues. Managers could profit personally from inflated contracts while facing minimal consequences for waste. There were many other similar cases of excess imports of deliberately substandard products at inflated prices to maximize foreign currency arbitrage (Reuters, 2011).

Reinhart and Santos (2016), based on the balance of payments published by the Venezuelan Central Bank, estimated that capital flight during the first eight years of the exchange control system (2003–2011) totaled $133.2 billion, equivalent to an average of 9–17% of Venezuelan GDP. As the authors conclude, the control was not imposed to put a halt to the capital flight but rather to decide who was allowed to fly.

In the long term, perhaps the most devastating economic consequence of exchange controls was the systematic destruction of Venezuela's productive capacity. Subsidized imports made it cheaper to import almost everything than to produce domestically, with the result that "many genuine businesses also specialized away from productive activities towards securing cheap dollars" (Economics Observatory, 2024). This "hamstrung domestic production, making the country extremely reliant on imports, even for products that Venezuela had previously exported, such as rice" (Fletcher, 2004). Industries that had operated for decades simply closed rather than compete with subsidized imports. World Bank data shows that manufacturing's contribution to GDP declined from approximately 16% in the early 2000s to just 12% by 2014, with the sector experiencing severe difficulties amid lack of investment (World Bank, 2024). The agricultural sector was particularly devastated. According to FAO statistics, Venezuela's agricultural self-sufficiency declined dramatically, with the country importing about two-thirds of its food needs by the 2010s (Food and Agriculture Organization, 2024).

The exchange control system became a primary driver of Venezuela's hyperinflation and food scarcity. Multiple exchange rates created parallel markets with wildly different prices for the same goods. By late 2018, the central exchange rate through the state-controlled DICOM auction system was 63.81 Sovereign Bolivars (VES) to 1 USD, while the black-market exchange rate was 171.34 VES to 1 USD - making life nearly three times more expensive without access to the official exchange rate (Adam Smith Institute, 2024). Corruption in subsidized food imports reached new heights at this time with the CLAP food distribution program (U.S. Department of the Treasury, 2019a).

United States' Treasury officials determined that "Venezuelan officials pocketed 70% of the proceeds allocated to import programs destined to alleviate hunger in Venezuela" (The Washington Post, 2018). Colombian authorities seized 25,200 CLAP boxes containing about 400 tons of decomposing food destined for the Venezuelan public (El Tiempo, 2018).

The cumulative impact over sixteen years of exchange controls was catastrophic. The Economics Observatory calculated that "Venezuela lost an estimated $300 billion to corruption through its foreign currency system and other schemes" between the early 2000s and mid 2010s. When oil prices collapsed from $100 to $40 per barrel in 2014, "Venezuela was drastically unprepared" due to aggressive pro-cyclical fiscal policy and lack of savings, exacerbated by the massive resource misallocation caused by exchange controls (Economics Observatory, 2024). The sixteen-year persistence of this system, from CADIVI's establishment in 2003 through DICOM's elimination in May 2019, demonstrates how entrenched rent-seeking interests can perpetuate economically destructive policies. The corruption was not peripheral but central to the system's operation. From the Pudreval food scandal to the CLAP program theft, from ghost companies importing nothing to systematic overpricing of real imports, the exchange control regime became a mechanism for wholesale looting of national resources.

### *The Long Process of Dismantling Foreign Exchange Controls*

The first meaningful step toward dismantling foreign exchange controls came with the establishment of the DICOM foreign currency auction system. Unlike previous exchange mechanisms, DICOM represented a fundamental shift toward market-based pricing while maintaining Central Bank oversight. The new system allowed private parties to buy and sell foreign currency through auctions administered by the Central Bank of Venezuela (Norton Rose Fulbright, 2017). The DICOM system immediately revealed the extent of currency overvaluation that had accumulated under the previous controls at official rates. The initial DICOM range between 1800 and 2200 bolivars per dollar represented "at least a 60 percent" devaluation from the previous SIMADI rate (Reuters, 2017b). This marked the beginning of a series of massive devaluations.

Weekly auctions sold approximately $30.3 million – a relatively low amount, indicating that while more flexible than its predecessors, the system still failed to meet market demand for foreign currency (Reuters, 2017a). A more crucial step toward dismantling the multitier system occurred in January 2018, when the heavily subsidized DIPRO exchange rate of 10 bolivars per dollar was eliminated (Reuters, 2018b). The unification of exchange rates at the DICOM level was accompanied by dramatic devaluations. Moreover, in August 2018, money exchange operations between private parties were legalized, effectively decriminalizing the parallel market for foreign currency (Reuters, 2018c). The decision effectively legalized what had become the de facto currency market for most Venezuelan economic activity.

By 2019, the exchange control system faced multiple pressures that made its continuation impossible. Sanctions had severely constrained the Central Bank's ability to operate international transactions, forcing the institution to resort to increasingly primitive methods. Reuters reported that "Venezuela's central bank has begun using piles of cash rather than electronic transfer to sell foreign exchange to local banks" (Reuters, 2019a). As a result, the DICOM's volumes had fallen to negligible levels. According to Central Bank data, the monetary authority had sold just $32 million through DICOM in the first months of 2019, compared to the billions needed to meet market demand (Reuters, 2019b). The system had essentially ceased functioning as a meaningful source of foreign currency for the Venezuelan economy.

The formal end of Venezuela's exchange control system came with a Central Bank resolution dated May 2, 2019, which created "exchange tables" (*mesas de cambio*) to be operated by Venezuelan banks (Venezuelanalysis, 2019). The central bank stopped offering any foreign currency for sale through DICOM by the end of April, following US sanctions on the institution (Reuters, 2019b). This formally marked the end of sixteen years of exchange controls in Venezuela.

## *Documenting Welfare Benefits of Eliminating Exchange Controls*

One of the main consequences of foreign exchange controls was the overpricing of Venezuelan imports. Overpriced imports were welfare reducing for macro, micro, institutional, and productive reasons. At a macro level, overpricing meant that Venezuela was losing foreign currency reserves at rates inconsistent with the goods that were being channeled into the country. At a micro level, overpricing led to insensibly high levels of wasteful imports, only noisily correlating with domestic demand. Institutionally, the overpricing opportunities led to corruption levels orders of magnitude beyond any regional benchmark. Finally, overpricing incentivized Venezuelan firms to redeploy their capabilities from production toward activities that eased their access to subsidized foreign currency.

To measure the levels of overpricing of Venezuelan imports, we leveraged customs data from Colombia, whose Customs and Tax Agency (*Direccion de*

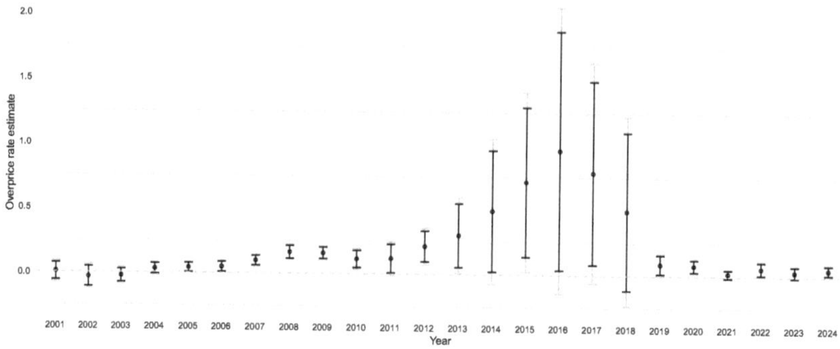


**Figure 17** Yearly Venezuelan import overprice estimates

**Note:** Figure shows yearly estimates of overpricing of Colombian exports to Venezuela in comparison to other importer countries between 2001 and 2024. Each point represents the coefficient from a year-specific regression following Equation 4. Log FOB prices are estimated as a function of a Venezuelan-importer indicator variable, controlling for firm-product-week fixed effects. The coefficient captures the average percent price difference when the same Colombian exporter sells the same product during the same week to Venezuela versus other countries. Dark and light gray vertical lines capture 90% and 95% confidence intervals. Observations are weighted by transaction value.

**Source:** Colombia's *Dirección de Impuestos y Aduanas Nacionales* (DIAN) transaction-level export data. Authors' calculations.

*Impuestos y Aduanas Nacionales*, DIAN) publishes transaction-level exports data between 2001 and 2024. This data allows us to observe the *freight on board* (FOB) prices of each Colombian export transaction during this period. Chiefly, we can also observe the specific product category of the exported good, the tax ID of the exporting company, the date of the transaction, and the destination country of all Colombian exports during this period. With these data, we can compare the export price differences of transactions of the same product, by the same firm during the same week, whenever the goods were being imported by Venezuela or when they were being imported by a different country.

We make this comparison separately for each year available in the data to estimate yearly average import overpricing rates. Figure 17 shows these estimates between 2001 and 2024, capturing two years before the start of foreign exchange controls, sixteen years of controls, and five years after the end of exchange controls. Overprice estimates are indistinguishable from zero until 2003, but they start growing immediately after, reaching 14% between 2008 and 2012. However, average overprices start to grow aggressively with the onset of the economic crisis, and peak at a whopping 96% in 2016. Overprices subside slightly in 2017, the year DICOM and financial sanctions were first enacted, reaching 78%. Overpricing, which averaged 49% in 2018, collapsed to 8% by 2019 with the end of foreign exchange controls. By 2021, overpricing had essentially disappeared. Additional details about our methods and estimates are in the Technical appendix for Case Study 4.

These results highlight several issues. As discussed earlier, the bulk of the collapse of the Venezuelan economy and of Venezuelan imports occurred between 2013 and 2016, before the enactment of the first financial sanctions of 2017. Far from eliminating import inefficiencies to address the ensuing crisis, the response of the Maduro regime seemed to aggravate overpricing imbalances in favor of well-connected importers. The growth in overpricing between 2013 and 2016 suggests that the import collapse during this period, usually measured in dollar terms, was probably steeper, if considered in terms of available imported items. Most importantly, average overprice levels dovetail with the evolution of foreign exchange controls, which were enacted in 2003, relaxed in 2017, and fully removed in 2019. Chiefly, the subsiding of overprice levels in 2017, and their collapse in 2019, coincide with the enactment of the 2017 and 2019 sanctions.

## 8 Reframing the Effects of Economic Sanctions on Venezuela: From Collective Punishment to Constraints on Authority

The preceding analysis has critically examined the dominant narrative that sanctions on Venezuela - in particular the financial sanctions imposed on August 2017 and the broader sanctions imposed on the oil sector on January 2019 - had disproportionate negative effects on economic activity, welfare outcomes and the humanitarian crisis. To test this proposition, we rely on a series of empirical analyses using high-frequency and spatially disaggregated data to test whether sanctions had significant, differential (from the impacts of other relevant, concurrent events) and incremental (to previously existing trends) negative effects on key welfare and economic outcomes as posited by the "collective punishment" framework. Across all dimensions examined, our findings challenge this narrative.

Three of our tests are meant to evaluate the notion that sanctions had an incremental negative impact on welfare via oil production. This is important because most of the empirical literature focuses on oil output as a proxy for welfare, without testing its impacts on other more direct outcomes, such as consumption. There are two channels by which sanctions could have negative impacts on welfare, lower public revenues available to support expenditure and social programs, and lower economic activity - volumes, employment, wages - in oil-producing municipalities. The former channel can be expected to affect all regions alike, under the reasonable assumption that lower public revenues force a widespread contraction in expenditure that is proportionally distributed across regions (not equally distributed, but proportionately, such that the share of public expenditure in social programs remains the same). The latter channel can only impact oil-producing regions. By definition, if sanctions had a disproportionate negative impact on welfare, we would expect that oil-producing areas will be differentially more affected. We test this hypothesis on three different outcomes by running event studies and difference-in-difference analyses on high frequency data contrasting oil-producing vs. non-oil-producing municipalities.

Using proprietary monthly data on per capita cornflour sales at the municipal level, we find no statistically significant decline in sales (consumption) in oil-producing regions relative to non-oil-producing regions following the imposition of financial sanctions in August 2017. Cornflour sales had already been declining prior to sanctions and in oil-producing areas they began to stabilize or improve after 2018. This finding is inconsistent with the claim that sanctions triggered an acute food consumption collapse in areas more dependent on oil rents.

Leveraging high-frequency VIIRS satellite data on nighttime luminosity, a widely accepted proxy for economic activity, we observe no disproportionate decline in light intensity in oil-producing municipalities relative to others post-2017. Both groups experienced a downturn consistent with preexisting trends, with no statistically significant divergence attributable to sanctions. These results reinforce the notion that sanctions did not induce a spatially concentrated economic contraction in oil-reliant regions.

Analyzing electoral turnout data across municipalities, we use the relative decline in turnout as a proxy for out-migration. If sanctions had triggered a localized refugee wave in oil municipalities, we would expect lower turnout in those areas. However, our difference-in-differences estimates show no statistically significant difference in turnout trends between oil and non-oil municipalities after sanctions. This contradicts the hypothesis that sanctions-induced economic hardship drove disproportionate emigration from oil-producing regions.

The fourth empirical analysis presented in this Element has a different nature: We exploit daily variation in oil production considering field-specific dependencies on external energy inputs. Specifically, we leverage proprietary data on daily, field-specific output from gas-lifted fields versus injection fields that rely more intensively on the domestic power supply. Focusing on the blackouts of 2019 - which occurred after the enactment of oil sanctions in 2019 - we find massive immediate effects that concentrate in, but are not exclusive to fields relatively dependent on access to electricity. This finding further undermines the hypothesis that oil sanctions were the primary driver of Venezuela's production collapse, providing specific evidence that concurrent treatments had massive independent effects. This confirms that assuming that oil production drops that occurred after the enactment of sanctions are a consequence of sanctions relies on a highly problematic identification strategy.

Taken together, these initial four empirical analyses challenge the prevailing narrative that US sanctions had a disproportionate negative impact on welfare and economic outcomes. These findings provide strong evidence against the hypothesis that sanctions were the primary cause of Venezuela's economic and humanitarian collapse.

We examine the evolution of essential imports and price markups on Colombian goods imported into Venezuela, which reflect both the key link between oil production and domestic living standards, and opportunities for rent extraction under the dual exchange rate system. These markups, especially on basic staples, were significantly larger prior to 2017, providing regime insiders with arbitrage rents. Our analysis shows that these markups began to decline following the 2017 financial sanctions and disappeared entirely after the 2019 oil sanctions. Relying on customs data, we also track the overpricing of Venezuelan imports across key product lines. Overpricing - used extensively to divert public foreign currency allocations - was a defining feature of Venezuela's import system under exchange controls. We find that the incidence of overpricing began to fall after 2017 and was largely eliminated following the collapse of the official foreign exchange allocation system in 2019.

How can it possibly be that sanctions, rather than deepening Venezuela's collapse, led to improvements across some key economic outcomes? The answer lies not in the sanctions themselves, but in the policy response they triggered. In an effort to cushion the impact of these external restrictions, the government was compelled to unwind a series of long-standing economic controls - measures that had constrained activity and distorted incentives for over fifteen years. This shift, though unplanned and politically reluctant, marked a significant departure, arrested the pace of decline, and created space for limited, localized improvements - particularly in areas where market forces were allowed to reemerge in practice, if not always in law.

These final two analyses explore a different, more tentative possibility: that the sanctions acted as a catalyst for policy changes which, although reluctant and partial, helped stabilize or improve some outcomes.

## Sanctions and the Unraveling of Economic Controls

The evidence presented in this Element suggests that the collapse of Venezuela's economy predated the imposition of sanctions. Most of the aggregates analyzed indicate that Venezuela hit rock bottom in 2016. By the end of that year, well ahead of the 2017 financial sanctions, the country had already experienced over 85% of the total GDP and import contraction that would eventually characterize its crisis. That context was further aggravated by the onset of hyperinflation, which, according to the Central Bank, officially began in December 2017, when monthly inflation surpassed the 50% threshold (55.6%).[25] Faced with a deepening collapse compounded by financial sanctions and hyperinflation, the government would eventually initiate a fundamental shift in economic policy, dismantling - at times de facto, at times de jure - the system of controls that had prevailed for more than fifteen years.

In late January 2018, the *Convenio Cambiario N°39* unified the exchange rates legally recognized by the government. In August 2018, the Constitutional Assembly proclaimed a year earlier as a parallel legislative body published a decree regarding "the annulment (*derogatoria*) of the exchange control and all illicit activities associated."[26]

On its motivation section, the decree announces the beginning of "a new regulatory framework whereby private agents can perform transactions in foreign currency in between them, with legal origin, without any limits other than those imposed by the law." Further to that, Articles 1 and 2 justify the elimination of the fifteen-year standing exchange control, "with the purpose of giving private agents, individual and firms, foreign and nationals, the amplest guarantee in the development of their activities within the socioeconomic model of the country."[27] Such language marked a profound departure from one of the core pillars of Chavismo's economic doctrine: its reliance on the monopoly and administration of foreign exchange as an instrument of political leverage and economic control.

Later that month, on August 17, 2018, Nicolas Maduro launched the "Program for Recovery, Growth and Economic Prosperity," an aggressive policy package aimed at curbing down inflation and stabilizing the economy. The policy package included a massive devaluation of the domestic currency, an increase in the Value Added Tax from 12% to 16%, and the announcement of the "activation" of 300 currency exchange offices (*casas de cambio*) across the country. Maduro also declared that deposits in foreign currency, as well as corresponding debit cards, would be introduced in the Venezuelan banking system, effectively normalizing dollar accounts for domestic use. Ironically,

---

[25] The start and end of Venezuela's hyperinflation episode follow the standard definition in the economic literature, which holds that hyperinflation begins when monthly price increases exceed 50% and ends when inflation remains below that threshold for twelve consecutive months (Cagan, 1956).

[26] Official Gazette N. 41.451, August 2nd, 2018

[27] For a complete legal and technical analysis of the *Convenio Cambiario N°39* and the decree published in the Official Gazette 41.451, see Hernandez (2021).

although the announcement was stressed to be aimed at "destroying the criminal dollar and the fixing and dollarizing of prices," what followed was a de facto dollarization of the economy.

These changes were galvanized from a legal standpoint with the publication of *Convenio Cambiario* 1 on September 7, 2018, which reestablished "free convertibility along the national territory in a market organized and regulated to guarantee its optimal functioning" (Article 1).[28] The departure from the longstanding exchange control is well captured in the wording of two articles that are noteworthy. Article 2 effectively eliminated the exchange control regime that had prevailed for fifteen consecutive years: "with the purpose of creating favorable conditions to the stability required for the functioning of the economy and the investment, free convertibility is reestablished along the national territory, *thereby ceasing all restrictions to exchange rate operations.*"[29] Article 9 establishes that, to all legal purposes, the exchange rate "will fluctuate freely according to the supply and demand of individuals and businesses, through the System of Market Exchange."[30]

In practice, *Convenio Cambiario 1* enabled the private sector to buy and sell foreign currency privately, without going through the Venezuelan Central Bank, including the free disposition of up to 80% of the foreign currency generated via exports.[31] It also established that there will be a single market exchange rate, that would fluctuate as a result of the free exchange of currency carried by the private sector through the authorized intermediaries. At last, it also authorized individuals over eighteen and legal entities to maintain foreign-currency deposits in Venezuelan financial institutions, without any requirements other than the standard anti–money laundering regulations (Article 32). In May 2019, months after oil sanctions were first announced, a Central Bank resolution finally allowed private banks to open accounts in foreign currency, removing remaining elements of the country's exchange control system (Reuters, 2019b).

These were not the only significant reforms introduced by the Venezuelan government under mounting external constraints. The liberalization of the foreign exchange regime rendered existing price controls, still formally

28 Extraordinary Official Gazette N. 6.405, September 7, 2018.

29 Italics added by the authors.

30 Article 9 also states that "The Central Bank will publish on its website the average exchange rate, weighted by the size of the operations carried in the System of Market Exchange," but the text of *Convenio Cambiario 1* does not include a description of such "System of Market Exchange."

31 Hernandez (2021), p. 75.

maintained under the Organic Law of Just Prices[32] increasingly irrelevant. In the context of hyperinflation and free-floating depreciating currency, from a practical standpoint the government effectively lost the capacity to update regulated prices with the frequency needed to keep pace with real market conditions. As a result, while the formal framework of maximum prices and punitive enforcement remains on the legal framework, in practice it became unenforceable: Actual market prices routinely exceeded the official ceilings, as increasingly more transactions started to occur in foreign currency.

Another striking example of this policy reversal came in June 2020, when the government formally dismantled the subsidy to domestic gasoline. On June 1, 2020, President Nicolás Maduro announced a new pricing system that combined a limited subsidy with a market-based, dollar-denominated tier for private consumption - marking the first time in decades that Venezuelans paid near-international prices for fuel. As Maduro himself declared during the televised address unveiling the plan, Venezuela would "no longer give away gasoline" (*Venezuela no va a regalar más gasolina*), framing the shift as a necessary adjustment under severe constraints.[33,34] The new structure allowed private individuals to purchase fuel at an unsubsidized rate of $0.50 per liter, while a subsidized quota was reserved for select users at a nominal price of $0.025 per liter, paid via local currency or foreign exchange. This partial liberalization stood in stark contrast to the decades-long policy of near-total fuel subsidization and underscored how external pressures and fiscal exhaustion compelled the government to retreat from one of its most iconic populist commitments.[35]

Crucially, this sweeping policy reversal did not reflect a change in convictions, but was rather imposed by necessity. It was not the product of ideological reorientation or paradigm shift but of material constraint. Regardless of intent, it is beyond dispute that these measures introduced elements of more efficient resource allocation and modestly improved the business climate within Venezuela's heavily distorted economy. Several authors have persuasively

---

32 The *Ley Orgánica de Precios Justos* was officially approved and implemented via Decreto-Ley No.600 on January 23, 2014, which took effect that same day through Gaceta Oficial No.40.340.

33 DW (2020) Maduro aumenta precio de la gasolina en Venezuela. Deutsche Welle, May 30. www.dw.com/es/maduro-aumenta-precio-de-la-gasolina-en-venezuela/a-53636483 (Accessed on June 29, 2025).

34 El País (2020) Maduro advierte a los venezolanos de que tendrán que volver a pagar la gasolina. El País, May 28. https://elpais.com/internacional/2020-05-28/maduro-advierte-a-los-venezolanos-de-que-tendran-que-volver-a-pagar-la-gasolina.html (Accessed on June 29, 2025).

35 See Barrios and Morales, 2012, for a detailed account of the cost of the gasoline subsidy in Venezuela.

argued that this reluctant liberalization was triggered by the financial sanctions imposed in August 2017 and further deepened by the broader sanctions targeting PDVSA in January 2019.

Palma (2020) is very explicit when it comes to the motivation behind the pivot toward market reforms observed from 2017 onward:

> *In the second half of 2018, and particularly in 2019, exchange controls were eased. This was due to the government's increasingly evident inability to continue imposing its unrestricted will on civil society in the process of allocating external resources. This incapacity arose fundamentally from the decline in oil revenues caused by the sustained contraction of production and export volumes, the fall in oil prices in recent years, and more recently,* ***the closure of the United States oil market as a result of the sanctions imposed by the United States government on PDVSA on January 21, 2019.*** *Also contributing to this incapacity were the reduction of international reserves, the elimination of the government's off-budget funds, and the constraints on obtaining international financing - limitations that were aggravated by United States financial sanctions against the Venezuelan public sector imposed in August 2017 and again in April 2019, in the latter case targeting the Central Bank of Venezuela.*[36]

Zambrano et al., 2021, in explaining the reasons behind their findings that the financial sanctions of August 2017 are associated with an increase in the value of monthly imports of food and medicine, argue that:

> *It can be argued that the government's change in policy orientation, which ultimately resulted in the loosening of the network of controls, was also an immediate consequence of the tightening of financial sanctions against PDVSA. In this case, the greater external availability of food and medicines would be a consequence of the sanctions policy, at least indirectly.*

Perhaps the more convincing argument supporting the notion that partial economic liberalization came as a response to sanctions imposed by the United States comes from Nicolas Maduro himself:

> *There is an American war room to sanction and destroy any effort Venezuela does to recover . . . Venezuela has the economic power, the industrial power, the wealth for us to circumvent these sanctions, this blockade . . . and stabilize its economy, real growth, and protect the social rights of our people . . . I am constantly vigilant to defend the currency, the bolivar, the salary, the incomes, with the carnet de la patria . . . evaluating all mechanisms, such as that process that some people call dollarization, may well serve the*

[36] Palma, P. (2020), p. 216. Translated by the authors.

> *recovery and redeployment of the productive forces of our country and the well functioning of the economy . . . it is a scape valve, thank God it exists.*[37]

## Sanctions as External Constraints on Absolute Authority

The core proposition advanced in this Element is that sanctions reshaped the Venezuelan political and economic landscape not primarily by imposing material deprivation, but by limiting the regime's capacity to exercise absolute discretion over key economic levers. The monopoly over the allocation of foreign exchange, the granting of import licenses, the provision of subsidize currency and credit, the capricious imposition, administration and sanctioning of maximum prices and profit margins - once instruments of patronage and control -became increasingly difficult to sustain. This loss of discretion, rather than furthering the economic collapse, induced a set of partial reforms that facilitated the reactivation of certain market mechanisms and mitigated further deterioration. While the evidence that sanctions did not cause Venezuela's collapse is robust and consistent, the claim that they helped improve outcomes through these constraints remains tentative, supported by suggestive patterns that warrant further investigation.

This dynamic reframes the impact of sanctions away from the "collective punishment" paradigm and toward a framework in which external constraints disrupt rent-distribution channels and force partial policy adjustments. These reforms did not amount to a transition to a free market economy, but they did mark a substantive departure from prior controls and were followed by observable improvements in welfare-relevant indicators, including the stabilization of imports, the partial recovery of output, the reduction in markups on tradables, and the disappearance of black-market arbitrage margins.

The Venezuelan experience demonstrates that the impacts of sanctions are not always straightforward or unidirectional. Their consequences depend critically on the political economy context, the institutional architecture of control, and the endogenous responses they trigger. In Venezuela, sanctions did not operate as collective punishment or as a cause of further economic collapse – for which we find no supporting evidence. Rather, they appear to have constrained the regime's authority in ways that compelled a reluctant unwinding of key pillars of its economic model.

[37] Maduro, N. (2019), YouTube video, Interview at Televen: José Vicente Hoy. November 17, 2019, minute 30:40 onwards, www.youtube.com/watch?v=vQT8srugE1A (Accessed on June 29, 2025).

From a policy perspective, this implies that the design of sanctions should pay closer attention to political economy dynamics–particularly how they interact with domestic institutions and reshape elite incentives. Sanctions that are broad enough to constrain discretionary fiscal authority yet carefully targeted to exacerbate internal contradictions–while still allowing humanitarian flows and preserving credible diplomatic channels–are more likely to yield leverage beyond mere symbolic condemnation. Without sanctions, or the credible threat of imposing or reimposing them, there is effectively no bargaining chip that can compel the Venezuelan regime to negotiate.

Sanctions, for all their costs, remain the only meaningful external lever because relief is the one concession the regime consistently demands. Absent this pressure, there is little incentive for substantive concessions. The Venezuelan case illustrates that sanctions did not cause further collapse but operated as an external constraint on authority that forced a reluctant regime to unwind long-standing pillars of its economic model. The reforms that followed, though partial and improvised, highlight a broader insight: Under certain conditions, sanctions may precipitate adaptive adjustments with nontrivial welfare effects.

# Appendix A

## A.1 Timeline of events

**Table A.1** Timeline of events, democratic backsliding, sanctions, and policy shifts

| Date | Event | Description |
|---|---|---|
| Mid 2013 | Onset of scarcity | Shortages of food and household goods become widespread, marking the visible start of Venezuela's prolonged economic and social collapse. |
| 2014 | Global oil price collapse | International oil prices fall by more than 50%, slashing Venezuela's export earnings and deepening the fiscal crisis of an oil-dependent economy. |
| 9 March 2015 | First individual United States sanctions | President Obama signs Executive Order 13692, imposing targeted sanctions on senior Venezuelan officials for corruption and human rights abuses. |
| 6 Dec 2015 | Opposition wins National Assembly | Opposition coalition secures a two-thirds supermajority in the National Assembly for the first time since Chávez came to power in 1998. |
| April 2016 | Supreme Court strips powers | TSJ declares the National Assembly in contempt and strips it of legislative authority, neutralizing the opposition's control. |
| Oct 2016 | Recall referendum blocked | National Electoral Council (CNE) suspends the opposition's constitutionally mandated recall referendum against Maduro. |

**Table A.1** (Cont.)

| | | |
|---|---|---|
| 29 March 2017 | National Assembly dissolved | TSJ formally dissolves the National Assembly's powers, triggering nationwide protests and international condemnation. |
| 30 July 2017 | Constitutional Assembly election | Disregarding constitutional requirements, Maduro's government holds elections for a new National Constitutional Assembly (ANC) to bypass the opposition-controlled legislature. |
| 25 Aug 2017 | Financial sanctions imposed | Trump administration issues Executive Order 13808, blocking Venezuela and PDVSA from issuing or trading debt in United States markets. |
| November 2017 | Militarization of the Oil Company (PDVSA) | Major General of the Venezuelan National Guard Manuel Quevedo is named President of PDVSA and Minister of Oil. Major labor shortages in PDVSA are covered by members of the military. Oil output continued to plummet. |
| January 2018 | Elimination of DIPRO exchange system | The heavily subsidized DIPRO exchange rate was eliminated, effectively unifying the official exchange rate. |
| 20 May 2018 | Contested presidential election | Maduro claims reelection in a vote widely denounced as fraudulent due to opposition bans and reports of coercion. |
| August 2018 | Decree to end exchange control | The Constitutional Assembly publishes a decree annulling the fifteen-year standing exchange control, allowing private legal foreign exchange transactions within limits imposed by law. |

**Table A.1** (Cont.)

| | | |
|---|---|---|
| August 2018 | Economic Recovery Plan launched | President Maduro announces the "Program for Recovery, Growth and Economic Prosperity," including a massive currency devaluation, VAT hike, and opening of currency exchange houses to normalize dollar circulation. |
| 7 Sept 2018 | Convenio Cambiario No. 1 issued | Formal legal framework reinstates free convertibility of currency nationwide, removes exchange restrictions, and legalizes foreign currency bank accounts for individuals and businesses. |
| 10 Jan 2019 | Term expires, power vacuum | Maduro's second term formally begins despite widespread non-recognition. National Assembly declares the presidency vacant under the Constitution. |
| 23 Jan 2019 | Guaidó sworn in | Juan Guaidó sworn in as interim president under Article 233; immediately recognized by the United States and regional allies. |
| 28 Jan 2019 | Oil sanctions imposed | US Treasury designates PDVSA, blocking oil exports and freezing state oil revenues abroad. |
| 7–10 March 2019 | Nationwide blackouts | Massive national electricity grid failure leaves the country without power for days, severely disrupting oil production and daily life. |
| 30 April 2019 | Failed military uprising | Guaidó's attempted uprising to oust Maduro collapses within hours; opposition figures forced into exile. |
| 5 Aug 2019 | Comprehensive embargo | Executive Order 13884 freezes all Venezuelan government assets under US jurisdiction and prohibits most transactions. |

**Table A.1** (Cont.)

| | | |
|---|---|---|
| Feb 2020 | Rosneft Trading sanctioned | United States sanctions Rosneft's subsidiary for brokering Venezuela's oil exports to circumvent existing restrictions. |
| April 2020 | Narco-terrorism indictments | US Department of Justice indicts Maduro and senior officials for narco-terrorism and corruption, offering a multimillion-dollar reward. |
| 1 June 2020 | Gasoline subsidy removed | Maduro announces partial liberalization of fuel prices for the first time in decades, ending the historic practice of fully subsidized gasoline and introducing near-market pricing for private consumption. |
| 26 Oct 2022 | Chevron license (GL 41) issued | Biden administration grants Chevron a limited license to resume oil operations in Venezuela in exchange for political concessions on opposition primaries and candidate participation. |
| 18 Oct 2023 | Broader sanctions relief (GL 44) | United States expands sanctions relief to cover oil, gas, and gold sectors, conditional on the release of political prisoners and guarantees of fair elections. |
| Dec 2023 | Renewed crackdown | Maduro regime arrests opposition campaign team and blocks candidates, triggering threats of reimposing full sanctions. |
| 22 April 2024 | González permitted to run | Under international pressure, the Maduro regime allows Edmundo González Urrutia to replace María Corina Machado as the opposition's presidential candidate. |

**Table A.1** (Cont.)

| | | |
|---|---|---|
| 28 July 2024 | Disputed presidential election | Edmundo González wins a clear majority, but Maduro refuses to concede amid fraud allegations; widespread international condemnation follows. |
| Jan 2025 | New sanctions imposed | The United States, EU, and the UK announce additional sanctions, raise the bounty on Maduro to $25 million, and target regime officials' assets. |
| March 2025 | Chevron license revoked (GL 41A) | OFAC revokes Chevron's wind-down license in response to continued democratic backsliding, reinstating stricter oil and financial sanctions. |

## A.2 Technical Appendix for Case Study 1

### *Data and Sources*

The data comes from four main sources. From publicly available data, we identify municipalities with oil-sector operations. We use a binary marker of local presence of oil activities as our treatment measure.

Nighttime lights are from NASA's Visible Infrared Imaging Radiometer Suite (VIIRS). This provides a measure of total nightlight radiance, which is aggregated to a month by municipality level, effectively providing a panel structure where we can observe each municipality across all months between 2015 and 2018 - we exclude information after January 2019 in order to focus the analysis on the effects of the financial sanctions of 2019. Cornflour sales originate from proprietary data on cornflour kilograms sales by municipality-month from a large food company that shall remain anonymous. Finally, we gather electoral data for all elections before 2024 from Venezuela's Consejo Nacional Electoral (CNE), while data on the 2024 elections comes from the ComandoConVenezuela. Data from both sources are available at the precinct level. We aggregated information at the municipality level to obtain electoral turnout rates by municipality for each election. We calculate turnout rates by calculating the ratio of votes cast, including null and invalid votes, divided by the number of registered voters. We focus our study on the elections of 2012, 2013, 2015, 2018, and 2024. While the opposition boycotted the 2018 election, we incorporate it to our analysis as it is the only national election that occurred between the enactment of the 2017 financial sanctions and the 2019 oil sanctions. Lastly, we take baseline municipality-level measures of local poverty rates, population density, and local regime support in the 2013 presidential elections from the 2011 population census and from CNE.

## Empirical Strategy

For our difference-in-differences analyses, we estimate the following equation:

$$y_{i,t} = \beta After_t \times Oil_i + \psi_i + \psi_t + \varepsilon_{i,t} \quad (1)$$

Where $y_{i,t}$ is the outcome of interest at time $t$ and municipality $i$, $After_t$ is an indicator variable equal to 1 for observations after July 2017, and $Oil_i$ is an indicator for municipalities where oil activities are present. Their interaction effectively serves as the difference-in-differences term. $\phi_i$ and $\phi_t$ capture municipality and period (month or election) fixed effects. Standard errors are clustered at the municipality level. We consider specifications controlling for the interaction between $After_t$ and a set of baseline municipality-level covariates (poverty, population density, and regime support levels).

Event-study figures are based on regression specifications with the following structure:

$$y_{i,t} = \sum_{p \neq b} \beta^p * 1[t = p] \times Oil_i + \psi_i + \psi_t + \varepsilon_{i,t} \quad (2)$$

Where $1[t = p]$ is an indicator variable for an observation is in specific period $p$. $\beta^p$ is estimated for all periods other than the baseline period $b$, which is July 2017 for nighttime lights and cornflour sales, and the 2015 election for electoral turnout rates. The event-study figures shown in the paper control for the interaction between period-specific indicators and the same set of baseline municipality-level covariates.

## Robustness Checks

In addition to the empirical strategy of a difference-in-difference framework and event study plots, we also conduct robustness checks for all three outcomes of interest. We estimate different permutations of equation 1, iterating over relevant elements in each specification. We begin by doing so for the nighttime lights outcome. The baseline specification consists of estimating Equation 1 without control variables, equivalent to the first column of Table 3. We then consider three changes to the baseline difference-in-differences specification: the inclusion of control variables, using a logarithmic transformation of the outcome variable, and including municipalities that are in Caracas. Figure A.18 plots the four coefficient estimates as well as 95% confidence bars. We perform the same analysis for the cornflour sales outcome. The baseline specification is

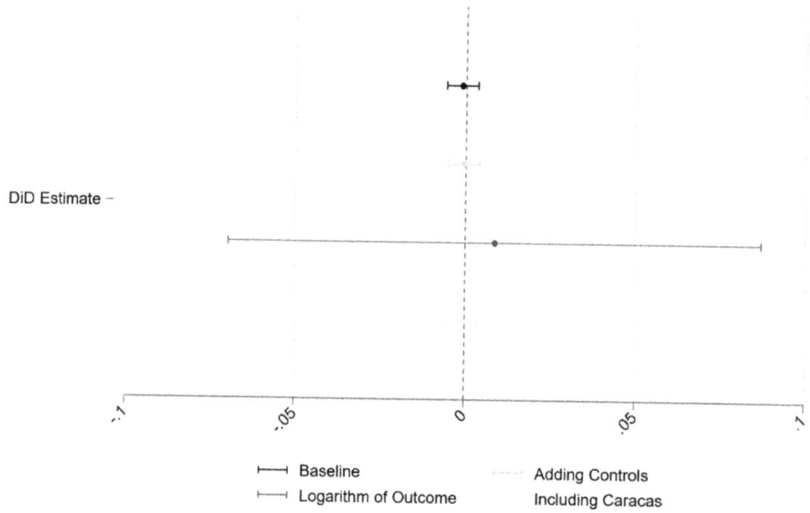


**Figure A.18** Coefficient plot - nighttime lights

**Note:** Difference-in-differences coefficient estimates and 95% confidence intervals for the effect of the August 2017 financial sanctions on nighttime light intensity in oil-producing versus non-oil-producing municipalities. Three specifications are shown: (1) Per capita nighttime lights excluding controls; (2) Per capita nighttime lights with additional controls for baseline population density, poverty rate, and regime support (2013 chavista vote share); (3) Log nighttime lights using total radiance; (4) Per capita nighttime lights including the Caracas metropolitan area municipalities. The difference-in-differences term is the interaction between a post-July 2017 indicator and an oil municipality indicator. All specifications include municipality and month fixed effects. Standard errors are clustered at the municipality level.

**Source:** NASA's Visible Infrared Imaging Radiometer Suite (VIIRS). Authors' calculations.

equivalent to column 3 in Table 3. Figure A.19 plots the four aforementioned changes in specification for cornflour sales. The results remain consistent.

Lastly, to ensure robustness of our turnout results, we also estimate different permutations of the specification in Equation 1. Our baseline specification includes all elections in the sample but excludes control variables, equivalent to column 5 of Table 3. We proceed to estimate turnout including control variables, including Caracas, including both controls and Caracas, excluding the 2018 election and excluding the 2024 election. Figure A.20 plots the six coefficient estimates for turnout rates. Once again, the estimates support our previous conclusions.

All of the robustness figures are consistent with the conclusions from the difference-in-differences estimates and the event study analysis. The results remain stable when Caracas is excluded or included, when alternative transformations of the dependent variables are employed, and when the sample

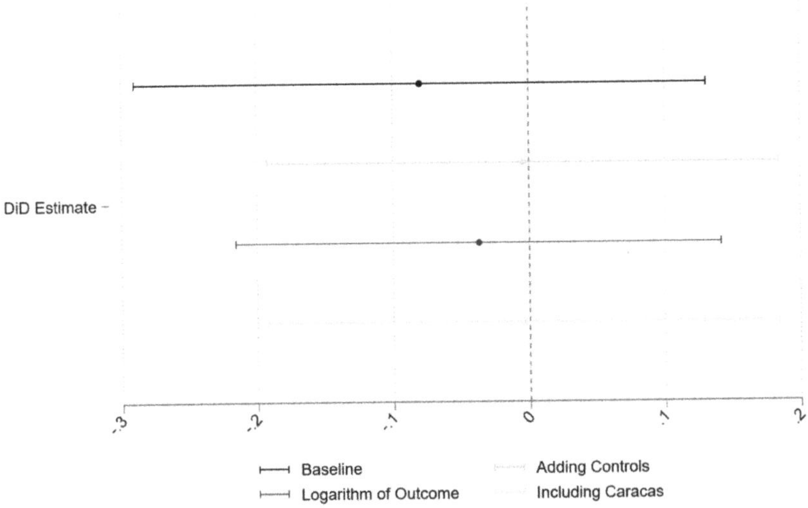


**Figure A.19** Coefficient plot - cornflour sales

**Note:** Difference-in-differences coefficient estimates and 95% confidence intervals for the effect of the August 2017 financial sanctions on cornflour sales in oil-producing versus non-oil-producing municipalities. Three specifications are shown: (1) Per capita cornflour sold excluding Caracas metropolitan area municipalities; (2) Per capita cornflour sold with additional controls for baseline population density, poverty rate, and regime support (2013 chavista vote share) (3) Log kilograms of cornflour; (4) Per capita cornflour sold including the Caracas metropolitan area municipalities. The difference-in-differences term is the interaction between a post-July 2017 indicator and an oil municipality indicator. All specifications include municipality and month fixed effects. Standard errors are clustered at the municipality level.

**Source:** Proprietary data from a large food producer in Venezuela. Authors' calculations.

is restricted by electoral cycle. The coefficient plots do not suggest statistically significant differences after the 2017 sanctions between oil and non-oil municipalities.

## A.3 Technical appendix for Case Study 2

### *Data Characteristics and Access Conditions*

For one week in January 2020, Morales-Arilla worked with the data used in this Element through a secured computer without access to the internet at the headquarters of an oil consulting firm that shall remain anonymous. The data had daily oil production information (in barrels) for each of the sixty-four oil fields in the Venezuela between January 1 and October 31, 2019. The data classified each field by technology group according to wether pumping steam into the oil field is required for extraction ("Pump" fields) or wether oil flows naturally due to the associated gas within the field ("Gas" fields). While generally known,

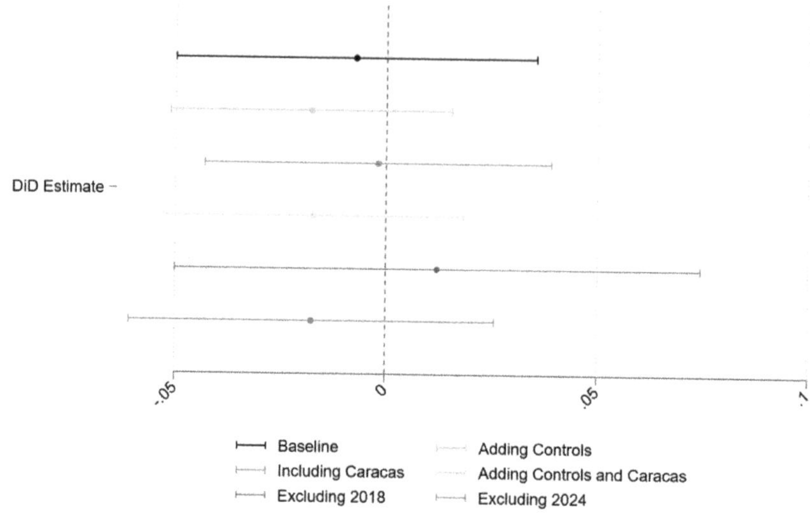


**Figure A.20** Coefficient plot - voter turnout

**Note:** Difference-in-differences coefficient estimates and 95% confidence intervals for the effect of the August 2017 financial sanctions on electoral turnout in oil-producing versus non-oil-producing municipalities. Three specifications are shown: (1) Turnout without control variables (2) Turnout with additional controls for baseline population density, poverty rate, and regime support (2013 chavista vote share); (3) Turnout including municipalities in Caracas; (4) Turnout including both controls and Caracas; (5) Turnout excluding the 2018 election; (6) Turnout excluding the 2024 election. The difference-in-differences term is the interaction between a post-July 2017 indicator and an oil municipality indicator. All specifications include municipality and month fixed effects. Standard crrors arc clustered at the municipality level.

**Source:** CNE and ComandoConVenezuela. Authors' calculations.

the relative importance of power supply for oil extraction in "Pump" fields was confirmed through discussions with engineering leaders at the consulting firm. As required by the firm, the author first transformed the data into field-specific indices of variation, based on the average production of each field during the first week of January, before any of the concurrent treatments under consideration (constitutional crisis, sanctions, protests, blackouts, failed coup attempt, etc.) had occurred. These field-specific indices were used to study the effects of blackouts on oil production.

## *Regression Discontinuity Specification*

We perform a standard regression discontinuity specification by estimating the following equation:

$$O_{fd} = \beta_0 + \beta_1 B_d + \beta_2 D_d + \beta_3 B_d * D_d + \epsilon_{fd} \tag{3}$$

Where $O$ is the oil production index of field $f$ on day $d$, $D_d$ is the number of days of day $d$ before or after March 07 (the day of the blackout), and $B_d$ is a binary marker for whether day $d$ occurs after the blackout, and $\epsilon_{fd}$ is the error term. While $\beta_2$ and $\beta_3$ capture the shape of a linear function between time and the average production indices before and after the blackouts, $\beta_1$ captures the estimated discrete change in average oil production indices on the day of the blackout. In estimating uncertainty, we cluster standard errors at the oil field level. Moreover, we follow Calonico et al. (2020) in estimating an optimal bandwidth period of two weeks around the start of blackouts. Moreover, we consider the recommendations in Hausman and Rapson (2018) for addressing the typical "mass" problems that often occur in regression discontinuities in time (RDiT) designs.

In order to assess heterogeneities according to field type, we first separated fields into a "Pump" fields group and a "Gas" fields group, and then estimated separate RDiT estimates of the effects of the blackouts. For these specifications, we do not reestimate optimal bandwidths, but use the same two weeks of the main specification. In unreported results, we show that negative and significant estimates are specific to the date of the blackouts, and that the aggregate and group-specific conclusions discussed earlier are robust to widening and narrowing the bandwidth and to considering quadratic functions around the day of the blackout.[38]

Moreover, in order to estimate the effect of the blackout in number of barrels considering the relative size of each field, we estimated RDiT effects specifically for each oil field in the country following the same specification and considering the same bandwidth discussed earlier. As expected due to precision losses in field-specific specifications, estimates are not statistically significant for sixteen out of the sixty-four oil fields. However, estimates for the majority of these cases are relatively close to 0. We take each field-specific estimate (expressed in percentage points from the early January reference) and multiply them their specific reference value to estimate field-specific barrel-per-day losses. We aggregate these estimates across fields to estimate losses of 728,000 barrels per day.

## Estimating Lowest-Possible Blackout-Induced Losses

As mentioned earlier, the fact that "Pump" fields started greatly underperforming "Gas" fields after the blackouts could be used to approximate the lowest-possible effects of power supply disruptions in 2019. We argue that

38 We focus on low-order polynomial functions around the discontinuity following the recommendations in Gelman and Imbens (2019).

this would be a "lowest possible" estimate because the calculation is based on the assumption that power supply disruptions do not affect production in "Gas" fields, something we know is not true given the lower, but still sizeable and significant, effects of the blackouts on oil production in "Gas" fields. Still, we find this approach to be informative of the potential first-order magnitude of the concurrent treatments that large portions of the literature on sanctions disregard.

We build field-specific daily production indices with a baseline determined by production levels during the first week of January. With these indices, we can assess how much worse the "Pump" fields are performing vis-a-vis "Gas" fields on a specific day after the start of the blackouts. We multiply that difference by the baseline production level in "Pump" fields to get a "lowest-possible" effects in terms of daily barrels of oil. We then collect total losses by multiplying the aggregate drop in the production index by the national aggregate production reference from early January. Finally, we multiply these aggregates by daily WTI oil prices in order to obtain a daily dollar estimate of these losses. Finally, we aggregate these losses cumulatively between January 1 and October 31. Following this approach, our estimate of the lowest-possible losses induced by the blackouts adds up to $2.3 billion - one-third of total estimated losses.

## A.4 Technical appendix for Case Study 3

We take import data by product for all countries in the world between 2012 and 2023 from Harvard's Atlas of Economic Complexity (Growth Lab at Harvard University, 2024). The data identifies traded items according to the 2012 Harmonized System (HS) product classification. Following Zambrano (2023), we define food items as those that have the first two digits of their HS product code take values below the value of 25, excluding 23, 13, 12, 05, and 0101. Similarly, we define medicines as items that have a value of 30 for the first two digits of their HS code. We aggregate import values for these products at the country-year level and create an index of essential imports by dividing values by the imports of their respective country in 2012 and multiplying by 100.

As discussed in the main body of the paper, we restrict the sample of potential donor countries by removing small and island nations as well as dependent territories, and by removing the set of countries that were exposed to sanctions or similar treatments from the United States in the period of analysis. We identify a synthetic counterfactual for Venezuela's essential import index, produce its relevant estimates, calculate estimates for placebo units, and estimate p-values for the statistical significance of post-treatment differences between Venezuela and its synthetic counterfactual using the "synth" and "synth_runner" packages in Stata (Abadie et al., 2011; Galiani and Quistorff, 2017; Yan and Chen, 2023).

In our preferred specification, we calculate the synthetic benchmark for Venezuela's essential import index fitting the algorithm to Venezuelan indices between 2013 and 2016 with a list of potential donors that excludes small nations, island nations and dependent territories, and excludes countries facing sanctions and other similar commercial restrictions from the United States (Russia, Syria, Cuba, North Korea, Iran, Sudan, Belarus, and Myanmar). We iterate our preferred specification along three dimensions: (1) Adding 2017 to the fitting period of the synthetic control algorithm, (2) using the natural logarithm of essential imports as the outcome variable, and (3) restricting the pool of potential donor countries to the list proposed in Rodríguez (2019) (Algeria, Argentina, Azerbaijan, Brazil, China, Colombia, Egypt, India, Indonesia, Kazakhstan, Malaysia, Mexico, and Vietnam). While the strength of pre-treatment fits weakens in alternative specifications, the main analytic conclusion that the bulk of the collapse in Venezuelan essential imports occurred before the 2017 financial sanctions were first enacted remains unchanged.

## A.5 Technical appendix for Case Study 4

We take transaction-level export data between 2001 and 2024 from Colombia's *Dirección de Impuestos y Aduanas Nacionales* (DIAN). Each transaction identifies the exporter firm, the importing country, the traded product, the date of the transaction, the freight on board (FOB) dollar value of the transaction, and the number of traded units. With the latter two variables we are able to build a per unit FOB price associated with each transaction. To produce year-specific estimates of Venezuelan import overpricing, we sequentially estimate the following regression for each of the years in the data:

$$P_t = \alpha + \beta V_c + \phi_{f,p,w} + \epsilon_t \tag{4}$$

Where $P_t$ is the natural logarithm FOB price associated with export transaction $t$, $V_c$ is an indicator variable for whether the importing country $c$ is Venezuela or not, $\phi_{f,p,w}$ is a fixed effect for each combination of firm $f$ exporting product $p$ on week $w$, and $\epsilon_t$ is a transaction-specific error term. The value of $\beta$ captures the average percent difference in Venezuelan import prices conditional on firm-product-week averages. One way to describe the value of $\beta$ is as the average percent difference in the price of transactions from the same Colombian exporter selling the same product during the same week of the year to a Venezuelan importer in comparison to a non-Venezuelan importer. For our regression specification, we weigh each observation by the FOB dollar value of the transaction in order to make estimates representative of the overall Colombian export basket and to prevent results from being biased by smaller transactions made by individuals and smaller firms.

# References


Alberto Abadie and Javier Gardeazabal. The economic costs of conflict: A case study of the Basque country. *American Economic Review*, 93(1):113–132, 2003.

Alberto Abadie, Alexis Diamond, and Jens Hainmueller. Synthetic control methods for comparative case studies: Estimating the effect of California's tobacco control program. *Journal of the American Statistical Association*, 105(490):493–505, 2010.

Alberto Abadie, Alexis Diamond, and Jens Hainmueller. Synth: Stata module to implement synthetic control methods for comparative case studies, statistical software components s457334. *Boston College Department of Economics*, 2011.

Adam Smith Institute. Venezuela campaign: The amazing corruption machine. www.adamsmith.org/blog/venezuela-campaign-the-amazing-corruption-ma chine, 2024.

Agencia EFE. Unos 170 millones de kilos de alimentos importados por venezuela se han vencido. *EFE*, July 2010.

Anadolu Agency. Venezuela's Maduro hinges talks with opposition on lifting of sanctions. *Anadolu Agency*, May 2021. www.aa.com.tr/en/americas/vene zuela-s-maduro-hinges-talks-with-opposition-on-lifting-of-sanctions/22555 53. Reports on Maduro's conditions for opposition talks linked to sanctions relief.

Asamblea Nacional. Declaración de usurpación de la presidencia y juramentación de juan guaidó. Caracas: Asamblea Nacional, 2019.

Dany Bahar. "su propio gráfico muestra que no hay tendencias paralelas antes del tratamiento entre los dos tipos de firma (un resultado que pone en duda la aplicabilidad del método)." Twitter, October 2024. https://x.com/dany_bahar/status/1914747944378552820. Tweet by @dany_bahar.

Dany Bahar and Ricardo Hausmann. Sanctions on Venezuela are not driving migration to the US southwest border: An empirical assessment. Working paper, Center for Global Development, 2025.

Dany Bahar, Carlos A Molina, and Miguel Angel Santos. Fool's gold: The impact of Venezuelan currency devaluations on multinational stock prices. *Economía*, 19(1):93–128, 2018.

Dany Bahar, Sebastian Bustos, José Ramón Morales-Arilla, and Miguel Angel Santos. Impact of the 2017 sanctions on Venezuela: Revisiting the evidence. Working paper, Brookings Institution, 2019.

Banco Central de Venezuela. Decreto no. 2302 sobre el régimen de administración de divisas. www.bcv.org.ve, 2003.

Bank for International Settlements. Foreign exchange market intervention in emerging markets: motives, techniques and implications. Technical Report BIS Papers No. 24, Bank for International Settlements, 2005.

Douglas Barrios and Miguel Ángel Santos. ¿ cuánto puede tomarle a venezuela recuperarse del colapso económico y qué debemos hacer? *Fragmentos de Venezuela. 20 escritos sobre economía*, page 91, 2017.

BBC News. Venezuela's Maduro recall referendum drive suspended. www.bbc.com/news/world-latin-america-37724322, 2016. October 21.

BBC News. Venezuela opposition leader Juan Guaidó declared interim president. www.bbc.co.uk/news/world-latin-america-47115857, 2019a. January 23.

BBC News. Venezuela power cut: Lootings as desperation grows. www.bbc.com/news/world-latin-america-47522208, 2019b. March 10.

BBC News. Venezuela crisis: Juan Guaidó calls for uprising as clashes erupt. www.bbc.com/news/world-latin-america-48114826, 2019c. April 30.

Bloomberg. Venezuela oil output slumps in first quarter as drilling slows. *Bloomberg*, May 2016. www.bloomberg.com/news/articles/2016-05-03/venezuela-oil-output-slumps-in-first-quarter-as-drilling-slows. News article on Venezuela's oil production decline in Q1 2016.

Deisy Buitrago, Vivian Sequera, and Matt Spetalnick. Venezuela, opposition sign election deal, paving way for US sanctions relief. *Reuters*, October 2023a. www.reuters.com/world/americas/venezuela-opposition-sign-election-deal-paving-way-us-sanctions-relief-2023-10-17/. Coverage of the Barbados agreement between Venezuelan government and opposition on electoral guarantees for 2024 elections.

Deisy Buitrago, Vivian Sequera, and Matt Spetalnick. Venezuela opposition will restart talks, us could ease sanctions. *Reuters*, October 2023b. www.reuters.com/world/americas/venezuela-opposition-will-restart-talks-us-could-ease-sanctions-2023-10-16/. Preview coverage of Venezuela-opposition talks resumption in Barbados with potential for US sanctions relief.

Nicolas Cabra-Ruiz, Sandra V Rozo, and Maria Micaela Sviatschi. Forced displacement, the perpetuation of autocratic leaders, and development in origin countries. Technical report, National Bureau of Economic Research, 2024.

Phillip Cagan. *The monetary dynamics of hyper-inflations*. PhD thesis, The University of Chicago, 1956.

Sebastian Calonico, Matias D Cattaneo, and Max H Farrell. Optimal bandwidth choice for robust bias-corrected inference in regression discontinuity designs. *The Econometrics Journal*, 23(2):192–210, 2020.

Javier Corrales and Dorothy Kronick. How Maduro stole Venezuela's vote. *Journal of Democracy*, 36(1):36–49, 2025.

Democracy Now! Economist Jeffrey Sachs: U.S. sanctions have devastated Venezuela & killed over 40,000 since 2017. May 2019. www.democracynow.org/2019/5/1/economist_jeffrey_sachs_us_sanctions_have. Interview with Jeffrey Sachs and Miguel Tinker Salas on Venezuela sanctions.

Economics Observatory. Why did Venezuela's economy collapse? 2024.

El Tiempo. Millonaria incautación de comida con gorgojo que iba a venezuela. *El Tiempo*, May 2018. Colombian authorities seize weevil-infested food destined for Venezuela's CLAP program.

Kimberly Ann Elliott. The sanctions glass: Half full or completely empty? *International Security*, 23(1):50–65, 1998. Defense of HSE findings against Pape's critique.

EU Council Decision. Council decision (cfsp) 2017/2074 concerning restrictive measures in view of the situation in Venezuela. https://eur-lex.europa.eu/eli/dec/2017/2074/oj/eng, 2017. Accessed: July 1, 2025.

Euronews. Eu no longer recognises juan guaidó as venezuela's interim president. www.euronews.com/my-europe/2021/01/07/eu-no-longer-recognises-juan-guaido-as-venezuela-s-interim-president, 2021. 7 January.

European Council. Declaration by the high representative on behalf of the EU on the parliamentary elections in Venezuela. www.consilium.europa.eu/en/press/press-releases/2020/12/07/venezuela-declaration-by-the-high-representative-on-behalf-of-the-european-union-on-the-elections-for-the-national-assembly/, 2020. Press Release, December 7.

European External Action Service. Venezuela: G7 foreign ministers' statement on presidential elections. www.eeas.europa.eu/eeas/venezuela-g7-foreign-ministers-statement-presidential-elections_en, 2024. July 31.

European Union Election Observation Mission. Venezuela regional and municipal elections 2021 – preliminary statement. www.eeas.europa.eu/eom-venezuela-2021_en, 2021. November 23.

Gabriel Felbermayr, T. Clifton Morgan, Constantinos Syropoulos, and Yoto V. Yotov. Understanding economic sanctions: Interdisciplinary perspectives on theory and evidence. *European Economic Review*, 135:103720, 2021. https://doi.org/10.1016/j.euroecorev.2021.103720. Comprehensive interdisciplinary review of sanctions literature in economics and political science.

Bruno Ferman, Cristine Pinto, and Vitor Possebom. Cherry picking with synthetic controls. *Journal of Policy Analysis and Management*, 39(2):510–532, 2020.

Financial Crimes Enforcement Network. Fincen advisory on widespread public corruption in venezuela. www.fincen.gov/sites/default/files/advisory/2020-09-21/FinCEN%20Advisory%20Venezuela%20FIN-2020-A006%20FINAL%20508.pdf, September 2020.

Erin Fletcher. *Bolívar Distorted: The Effects of Exchange Controls on the Venezuelan Economy*. PhD thesis, Duke University, 2004.

Food and Agriculture Organization. Faostat - food and agriculture data. www.fao.org/faostat/en/#country/236, 2024.

Foreign Policy. Maduro vs. guaidó: A global scorecard. https://foreignpolicy.com/2019/02/06/maduro-vs-guaido-a-global-scorecard-map-infographic/, 2019. February 6.

Fox News. Economist, prominent UN figure blames american sanctions for thousands of deaths in Venezuela. May 2019. https://www.foxnews.com/politics/economist-prominent-un-figure-blames-america-for-thousands-of-deaths-in-venezuela. News article covering Jeffrey Sachs and Mark Weisbrot's CEPR report on Venezuela sanctions.

Sebastian Galiani and Brian Quistorff. The synth_runner package: Utilities to automate synthetic control estimation using synth. *The Stata Journal*, 17(4):834–849, 2017.

Andrew Gelman and Guido Imbens. Why high-order polynomials should not be used in regression discontinuity designs. *Journal of Business & Economic Statistics*, 37(3):447–456, 2019.

Global Affairs Canada. Canada recognizes the interim president of Venezuela. www.canada.ca/en/global-affairs/news/2019/01/canada-recognizes-the-interim-president-of-venezuela.html, 2019. January 24.

Growth Lab at Harvard University. The atlas of economic complexity. Web application, 2024. https://atlas.hks.harvard.edu.

Grupo de Lima. Communique by the lima group 6th, meeting of the Lima group, may 14, 2018.

Jerg Gutmann, Matthias Neuenkirch, and Florian Neumeier. Precision-guided or blunt? the effects of US economic sanctions on human rights. *Public Choice*, 185(1):161–182, 2020.

Catherine Hausman and David S Rapson. Regression discontinuity in time: Considerations for empirical applications. *Annual Review of Resource Economics*, 10(1):533–552, 2018.

Ricardo Hausmann and Frank Muci. Don't blame washington for venezuela's oil woes: A rebuttal. *Americas Quarterly*, May 2019. www.americasquarterly.org/article/dont-blame-washington-for-venezuelas-oil-woes-a-rebuttal/.

Igor Hernández and Francisco Monaldi. Weathering collapse: An assessment of the financial and operational situation of the Venezuelan oil industry. *CID Working Paper Series 2016.327*, 2016.

José Ignacio Hernández. Control de cambio y de precio en Venezuela: Auge y colapso institucional (2003-2020): Del modelo socialista a la dolarización de facto. Number 146 in Colección Estudios Jurídicos. Editorial Jurídica Venezolana, Caracas, 2021. ISBN 978-1-68564-730-8.

José Ignacio Hernández. ¿y qué pasó con la licencia a chevron?, 2022. https://energiesnet.com/espanol/y-que-paso-con-la-licencia-a-chevron-jose-ignacio-hernandez-g-lga/.

Albert O Hirschman. *Exit, voice, and loyalty: Responses to decline in firms, organizations, and states*. Harvard University Press, Cambridge, MA, 1970. ISBN 0674276604.

Gary Clyde Hufbauer, Jeffrey J. Schott, Kimberly Ann Elliott, and Barbara Oegg. *Economic Sanctions Reconsidered*. Peterson Institute for International Economics, 2007.

HuffPost. Venezuela vota entre colegios y calles vacías, puntos de control del voto y bonos por meter la papeleta. www.huffingtonpost.es/2018/05/20/venezuela-vota-entre-colegios-y-calles-vacios-puntos-de-control-del-voto-y-bonos-por-meter-la-papeleta_a_23439434/, 2018. Accessed: 2 July 2025.

Nicolás Idrobo. Why economic sanctions backfire: The role of emigration in the Venezuelan case. *Available at SSRN 4930490*, 2024.

IMF. *World Economic Outlook, April 2015: Uneven Growth*. International Monetary Fund, 2015.

Infobae. Los 9 países que reconocieron la fraudulenta reelección de nicolás maduro a pesar del masivo repudio internacional. www.infobae.com/america/venezuela/2018/05/22/los-9-paises-que-reconocieron-la-fraudulenta-reeleccion-de-nicolas-maduro-a-pesar-del-masivo-repudio-internacional/, 2018. Accessed: July 2, 2025.

Itempnews Project. U.S. prosecutors on trail of $700 million in bribes to Venezuela's former treasurer. https://itempnews.org/2022/09/27/venezuela-treasurer/, 2022.

Andreina Itriago Acosta. Venezuela's opposition proposing sanction relief to woo maduro. *Bloomberg*, January 2022. www.bloomberg.com/news/articles/2022-01-28/venezuela-s-opposition-proposing-sanction-relief-to-woo-maduro. Reports on opposition proposal to ease US sanctions to bring Maduro back to negotiations, according to Juan Guaidó.

William H Kaempfer and Anton D Lowenberg. The political economy of economic sanctions. *Handbook of defense economics*, 2:867–911, 2007.

Ohyun Kwon, Constantinos Syropoulos, and Y Yotov. Pain and gain: The short-and long-run effects of economic sanctions on growth. *www.semanticscholar.org/paper/Painand-Gain%3A-The-Short-and-Long-run-Effects-of-on-Kwon-Syropoulos/72e2f76cc08e84ca374223e813b009588caba679*, 2020.

Juan Carlos Lamas. Books or bread: Venezuelan families struggle to afford school supplies. CGTN America, September 2017. https://america.cgtn.com/2017/09/23/books-bread-venezuela-school-families.

Manuel Llorens. Dolor país, versión venezuela. *Nueva Sociedad. N*, 274, 2018.

Jiaxuan Lu. Synthetic control method. In *Stata China Users Group Meeting*, China, August 2021. Stata. www.stata.com/meeting/china21-Uone-Tech/slides/China21_Jiaxuan.pdf. Conference presentation slides.

Jose Morales-Arilla. *Essays on the Political Economy of Development*. PhD thesis, Harvard University, 2022.

Jose Morales-Arilla and Jared Abbott. Captured participatory institutions in non-democracies: Theory and evidence from Venezuela's consejos comunales. *Available at SSRN*, 2024.

Jose Morales-Arilla and Salvador Traettino. Vulnerability, fear of retaliation and clientelism: Organizer identity and the backfire of solidarity. *Fear of Retaliation and Clientelism: Organizer Identity and the Backfire of Solidarity*, 2024.

Jose Morales-Arilla, Diego Martin, and Alvaro Morales. Escaping from hardship, searching for comfort: Climate matching in refugees' destination choices. *Journal of Development Economics*, 103500, 2025.

José Ramón Morales-Arilla. Sanciones: ¿causa o consecuencia de la crisis? Prodavinci, 2019.

Matthias Neuenkirch and Florian Neumeier. The impact of UN and US economic sanctions on gdp growth. *European Journal of Political Economy*, 40:110–125, 2015.

Matthias Neuenkirch and Florian Neumeier. The impact of US sanctions on poverty. *Journal of Development Economics*, 121:110–119, 2016.

Matthias Neuenkirch and Florian Neumeier. The economic effects of international sanctions: An event study. *Journal of Comparative Economics*, 51(4):1214–1231, 2023. https://doi.org/10.1016/j.jce.2023.06.003. Event study approach analyzing dynamic effects of sanctions.

Norton Rose Fulbright. Venezuela's new currency exchange law. Technical report, Norton Rose Fulbright, 2014.

Norton Rose Fulbright. Venezuela regulates new dicom system on auctions of foreign currency as part of the exchange control regime. Technical report, Norton Rose Fulbright, May 2017. Legal analysis of Exchange Agreement No. 38 and Resolution No. 17-05-01, published May 19, 2017.

Luis Oliveros. Efecto de las sanciones financieras y petroleras sobre venezuela. Report, Washington Office on Latin America, October 2020. www.wola.org/wp-content/uploads/2020/10/Oliveros-Resumen-FINAL.pdf.

Organization of American States. Press release: Oas permanent council agrees to not recognize the legitimacy of Nicolas Maduro's new term, 2021. Accessed: July 2, 2025.

Organization of the Petroleum Exporting Countries (OPEC). Annual statistical bulletin, 59th edition. https://publications.opec.org/asb/chapter/show/123/2104/2107, 2024. Annual Statistical Bulletin (ASB). OPEC, Vienna. ISSN: 0475-0608.

Pedro A. Palma. 1992-2022: Treinta años de experimentación cambiaria. 2020.

Robert A. Pape. Why economic sanctions do not work. *International Security*, 22(2):90–136, 1997. https://doi.org/10.1162/isec.22.2.90. Influential critique challenging the effectiveness of economic sanctions.

Robert A. Pape. Why economic sanctions still do not work. *International Security*, 23(1):66–77, 1998. Follow-up response defending original findings against Elliott's critique.

European Parliament. Resolution on the elections in Venezuela, 2018. May 3. (2018/2695(RSP)).

RealClearPolitics. Rep. ilhan omar: U.s. policies, "bullying" have led to the devastation in venezuela. RealClearPolitics, May 2019. www.realclearpolitics.com/video/2019/05/02/rep_ilhan_omar_us_policies_bullying_have_led_to_the_devastation_in_venezuela.html. Video and transcript of Rep. Ilhan Omar's Democracy Now! interview on Venezuela sanctions.

Carmen M Reinhart and Miguel Angel Santos. From financial repression to external distress: The case of Venezuela. *Emerging Markets Finance and Trade*, 52(2):255–284, 2016.

Reuters. Special report: Pension scandal shakes up Venezuelan oil giant. 2011.

Reuters. Venezuela's dicom exchange rate eases 17 percent to 2,640 bolivars per dollar. June 2017a. Documents early DICOM rate movements and trading volumes.

Reuters. Venezuela sets new exchange mechanism, as currency continues to slide. May 2017b. Reports initial DICOM launch with 60% devaluation from SIMADI rate.

Reuters. U.S. will not recognize venezuela election result: State department. www.reuters.com/article/us-argentina-g20-sullivan-idUSKCN1IL0QS, 2018. Accessed: July 2, 2025.

Reuters. Special report: Oil output goes awol in venezuela as soldiers run pdvsa. *Reuters*, December 2018a. www.reuters.com/article/us-venezuela-pdvsa-military-specialrepor/special-report-oil-output-goes-awol-in-venezuela-as-soldiers-run-pdvsa-idUSKCN1OP0RZ/. Special report on military management of Venezuela's state oil company.

Reuters. Venezuela eliminates heavily subsidized dipro forex rate. January 2018b. Reports elimination of 10 bolivar per dollar DIPRO rate and unification at DICOM.

Reuters. Venezuela's constituent assembly legalizes money exchanges. August 2018c. Reports decriminalization of parallel currency market operations.

Reuters. Venezuela enters fourth day of blackout as Maduro blames u.s. for power outage. www.reuters.com/article/idUSL1N20X044/, 2019. March 10.

Reuters. Hemmed in by sanctions, Venezuela central bank moves forex operations to cash. May 2019a. Documents primitive cash-based operations due to sanctions isolation.

Reuters. Venezuela loosens currency exchange controls to allow forex trading. May 2019b. Reports Central Bank resolution creating exchange tables and DICOM cessation.

Francisco Rodríguez. Crude realities: Understanding Venezuela's economic collapse. Report, Washington Office on Latin America, 2018.

Francisco Rodríguez. Sanctions and the Venezuelan economy: What the data say. Working paper, Torino Capital, 2019.

Francisco Rodríguez. Toxic conflict: Understanding Venezuela's economic collapse. Working paper, University of Notre Dame, 2021.

Francisco Rodríguez. The economic determinants of Venezuela's hunger crisis. Working paper, 2022a.

Francisco Rodríguez. Sanctions and imports of essential goods: A closer look at the equipo anova (2021) results. Working paper, 2022b.

Francisco Rodríguez. Sanctions and oil production: Evidence from Venezuela's orinoco basin. *Latin American Economic Review*, 31:1–31, 2022c.

Francisco Rodríguez. Sanctions, economic statecraft and Venezuela's crisis. Case study, Fourth Freedom Forum, 2022d.

Francisco Rodríguez. The human consequences of economic sanctions. *Journal of Economic Studies*, 51(4): 942–963, 2023.

Francisco Rodríguez. How economic sanctions affect human development: Evidence and policy implications. *Journal of Human Development and Capabilities*, 25(3): 499–504, 2024.

Francisco Rodríguez. *The Collapse of Venezuela: Scorched Earth Politics and Economic Decline, 2012-2020*. Kellogg Institute Series on Democracy and Development. University of Notre Dame Press, Notre Dame, IN, 2025a. ISBN 9780268209018.

Francisco Rodríguez. Sanctions and Venezuelan migration. Working paper, 2025b.

Luis Alejandro Ruiz. A negotiation focused on who cuts off whose head is not going to lead to an agreement. Interview, June 2025. https://guacamayave.com/en/francisco-rodriguez-a-negotiation-focused-on-who-cuts-off-whose-head-is-not-going-to-lead-to-an-agreement/.

Jeffrey Sachs and Mark Weisbrot. Punishing civilians: U.S. sanctions on venezuela. *Challenge*, 2019.

Miguel Santos. Venezuela: Running en empty. In *Lasa Forum*, volume 48, 2017.

Miguel Ángel Santos. La venezuela del día después (y la del día de antes). *Comunidad Venezuela: una agenda de investigación y acción local*, pages 44–65, 2021.

TalCual Digital. ¿fue legítima la convocatoria a una asamblea constituyente por nicolás maduro en 2017? https://talcualdigital.com/fue-legitima-la-convocatoria-a-una-asamblea-constituyente-por-nicolas-maduro-en-2017/, 2019.

The Washington Post. U.s. officials: 16 nations agree to track venezuela corruption. *The Washington Post*, April 2018.

Transparencia Venezuela. What happened with the cadivi case? https://transparenciave.org/project/what-happened-with-the-cadivi-case/, 2021.

TSJ. Sentencia no.156: Asunción de funciones legislativas de la Asamblea Nacional. https://pandectasdigital.blogspot.com/2017/03/sentencia-n-156-de-fecha-29-de-marzo-de.html, 2017. March 29th. Accessed July 1st, 2025.

TSJ. Sentencia no.260: Suspensión de proclamación de diputados electos del estado amazonas. http://historico.tsj.gob.ve/decisiones/selec/diciembre/184227-260-301215-2015-2015-000146.HTML, 2015. December 30.

TSJ. Sentencia no.1: Desincorporación de los diputados del estado amazonas. http://historico.tsj.gob.ve/decisiones/selec/enero/184253-1-11116-2016-X-2016-000001.HTML, 2016a. January 11.

TSJ. Sentencia no. 269: Desacato de la asamblea nacional. http://historico.tsj.gob.ve/decisiones/scon/junio/188317-473-14616-2016-11-0373.HTML, 2016b. Caracas: TSJ. Accessed: July 1, 2025.

UNHCR. Refugees and migrants from Venezuela top 4 million. www.unhcr.org/news/press/2019/6/5cfa2a4a4/refugees migrants venezuela top 4 million unhcr iom.html, 2019. UNHCR News, June 7.

UNHCR. United Nations High Commissioner for Refugees. Global trends: Forced displacement in 2023. www.unhcr.org/media/global-trends-report-2023, 2024. Accessed: July 1, 2025.

UNHCR. Emergency appeal: Venezuela situation. www.unhcr.org/us/emergencies/venezuela-situation, 2025. Accessed: July 1, 2025.

United States Department of Justice. Odebrecht and braskem plead guilty and agree to pay at least $3.5 billion in global penalties to resolve largest foreign bribery case in history. www.justice.gov/archives/opa/pr/odebrecht-and-braskem-plead-guilty-and-agree-pay-least-35-billion-global-penalties-resolve, December 2016. Office of Public Affairs press release documenting $788 million in bribes across 12 countries.

United States Department of Justice. Former Venezuelan national treasurer sentenced to 10 years in prison for money laundering conspiracy involving over $1 billion in bribes. www.justice.gov/opa/pr/former-venezuelan-national-treasurer-sentenced-10-years-prison-money-laundering-conspiracy, 2019.

United States Department of Justice. Nicolás Maduro moros and 14 current and former Venezuelan officials charged with narco-terrorism, corruption, drug trafficking and other criminal charges. www.justice.gov/archives/opa/pr/nicol-s-maduro-moros-and-14-current-and-former-venezuelan-officials-charged-narco-terrorism, 2020.

U.S. Department of State. Venezuela - investment climate statement. https://2009-2017.state.gov/e/eb/rls/othr/ics/2015/241792.htm, 2015.

U.S. Department of State. Recognition of Juan Guaidó as Venezuela's interim president. https://2017-2021.state.gov/recognition-of-juan-guaido-as-venezuelas-interim-president/, 2019. January 23.

U.S. Department of State. Fraudulent Venezuelan parliamentary elections. https://ar.usembassy.gov/the-united-states-condemns-venezuelas-fraudulent-legislative-elections/, 2020. Press Statement, December 6.

U.S. Department of State. Joint statement on Venezuela election. https://2021-2025.state.gov/joint-statement-on-venezuela-election/, 2024. August 16.

U.S. Department of the Treasury. Treasury sanctions Venezuela's state-owned oil company petroleos de venezuela, s.a. https://home.treasury.gov/news/press-releases/sm594.

U.S. Department of the Treasury. Treasury disrupts corruption network stealing from Venezuela's food distribution program, clap. https://home.treasury.gov/news/press-releases/sm741, 2019a.

U.S. Department of the Treasury. Treasury targets Venezuela currency exchange network scheme generating billions of dollars for corrupt regime insiders. https://home.treasury.gov/news/press-releases/sm583, 2019b.

U.S. DOJ. Nicolás Maduro Moros and 14 current and former venezuelan officials charged with narco-terrorism, corruption, drug trafficking and other criminal charges. www.justice.gov/archives/opa/pr/nicol-s-maduro-moros-and-14-current-and-former-venezuelan-officials-charged-narco-terrorism, 2020. DOJ Press Release, March 26.

U.S. Mission to the OAS. Assistant secretary nichols addresses the OAS permanent council on elections in Venezuela. https://usoas.usmission.gov/assistant-secretary-nichols-addresses-the-oas-permanent-council-on-elections-in-venezuela/, 2024. May 27.

U.S. Treasury. Executive order 13808: Imposing additional sanctions with respect to venezuela. www.federalregister.gov/documents/2017/08/29/2017-18468/imposing-additional-sanctions-with-respect-to-the-situation-in-venezuela, 2017. August 25.

U.S. Treasury. Treasury targets additional russian oil brokerage firm for continued support of Maduro regime, 2020. https://home.treasury.gov/news/press-releases/sm937.

U.S. Treasury. General license no. 41: Chevron corporation. https://ofac.treasury.gov/media/929531/download?inline, 2022. October 26.

U.S. Treasury. General license no. 44: Authorizing transactions related to oil and gas operations in venezuela. https://ofac.treasury.gov/media/932231/download?inline, 2023. October 18.

U.S. Treasury. Frequently asked questions related to the suspension of certain U.S. sanctions with respect to Venezuela on october 18, 2023 (updated april 17 2024). https://home.treasury.gov/news/press-releases/jy2234, 2024. Accessed: July 2, 2025.

Yolanda Valery. Venezuela: escándalo por alimentos vencidos. *BBC Mundo*, June 2010.

Venezuelan Electoral Council. 2021 election results archive. https://web.archive.org/web/20190607200303/http://www.cne.gov.ve/ResultadosElecciones2018/index.php, 2021. Accessed: July 2, 2025.

Venezuelanalysis. Venezuelan central bank liberalizes forex operations. May 2019. Analysis of May 2019 Central Bank resolution and expert commentary from Luis Salas.

White House. Executive order 13692. blocking property and suspending entry of certain persons contributing to the situation in Venezuela. www.presidency.ucsb.edu/documents/executive-order-13692-blocking-property-and-suspending-entry-certain-persons-contributing, 2015. 8 March. Washington, DC: The White House.

White House. Executive order 13884 of August 5, 2019 – blocking property of the government of venezuela. https://trumpwhitehouse.archives.gov/presidential-actions/executive-order-blocking-property-government-venezuela/, 2019. Federal Register, 84 FR 38843.

World Bank. *World development indicators: Venezuela.* 2021.

World Bank. World development indicators - manufacturing, value added (% of gdp). https://data.worldbank.org/indicator/NV.IND.MANF.ZS?locations=VE, 2024.

World Bank. Oil rents (% of gdp): Venezuela. https://data.worldbank.org/indicator/NY.GDP.PETR.RT.ZS?locations=VE, 2025. Data from World Development Indicators.

Guanpeng Yan and Qiang Chen. synth2: Synthetic control method with placebo tests, robustness test, and visualization. *The Stata Journal*, 23(3):597–624, 2023.

Omar Zambrano. Thread on imports after the 2019 oil sanctions. Twitter, February 2023. https://x.com/Econ_Vzla/status/1624121073737269292. Twitter thread by @Econ_Vzla.

Omar Zambrano, Hugo Hernández, Lisseth Escalante et al. Impacto de las sanciones financieras internacionales contra venezuela: Nueva evidencia. Policy brief, ANOVA Policy Research, 2021.

# Acknowledgements

We are deeply grateful to the editor and referees for their thorough review of this manuscript. Their detailed comments and constructive suggestions significantly strengthened our argument, sharpened our empirical strategy, and helped clarify the logic of our causal inference. We also want to thank seminar and workshop participants at the Harvard Growth Lab, the School of Government and Public Transformation at Tecnologico de Monterrey and the Department of Political Science at Texas A&M. The usual disclaimers apply.

# Cambridge Elements

# Economics of Emerging Markets

Bruno S. Sergi
*Harvard University*

Editor Bruno S. Sergi is an Instructor at Harvard University, an Associate of the Harvard University Davis Center for Russian and Eurasian Studies and Harvard University Asia Center. He is the Academic Series Editor of the Cambridge *Elements in the Economics of Emerging Markets* (Cambridge University Press), a co-editor of the *Lab for Entrepreneurship and Development* book series, and associate editor of *The American Economist*. Concurrently, he teaches International Political Economics at the University of Messina, Scientific Director of the Lab for Entrepreneurship and Development (LEAD), and a co-founder and Scientific Director of the International Center for Emerging Markets Research at RUDN University in Moscow. He has published over 200 articles in professional journals and twenty-one books as author, co-author, editor, and co-editor.

## About the Series

The aim of this Elements series is to deliver state-of-the-art, comprehensive coverage of the knowledge developed to date, including the dynamics and prospects of these economies, focusing on emerging markets' economics, finance, banking, technology advances, trade, demographic challenges, and their economic relations with the rest of the world, as well as the causal factors and limits of economic policy in these markets.

Cambridge Elements

# Economics of Emerging Markets

## Elements in the Series

*Harnessing Sovereign Wealth Funds in Emerging Economies toward Sustainable Development*
Mona Mostafa El-Sholkamy and Mohammad Habibur Rahman

*The Emerging Economies under the Dome of the Fourth Industrial Revolution*
Mark Esposito and Amit Kapoor

*On the Road to Economic Prosperity: The Role of Infrastructure in Ghana*
Tuan Anh Luong and Zenas Azuma

*Banking Stability and Financial Conglomerates in European Emerging Countries*
Pavla Klepková Vodová, Iveta Palečková and Daniel Stavárek

*The Paradox of Gender Equality and Economic Outcomes in Sub-Saharan Africa: The Role of Land Rights*
Evelyn F. Wamboye

*Mobile Banking and Access to Public Services in Bangladesh: Influencing Issues and Factors*
M. Kabir Hassan, Jannatul Ferdous and Hasanul Banna

*BRICS and the Global Financial Order: Liberalism Contested?*
Johannes Petry and Andreas Nölke

*Global South Leadership Style: Strategies for Navigating Emerging Economies*
Abel Femi Adekola, Mona Pearl, Bruno S. Sergi and Richard Muszynski III

*Islamic Finance and Sustainable Development*
M. Kabir Hassan, Aishath Muneeza and Rashedul Hasan

*Public-Private Dialogs to Spur Export-led Growth: The Case of Productivity Taskforces in Namibia*
Andrés Fortunato and Miguel Angel Santos

*Digitalization in Emerging Economies*
Mark Esposito, Yusaf Akbar and Frank Campbell

*From Collective Punishment to Constraints on Authority: Rethinking the Impact of US Sanctions on Venezuela*
Miguel Angel Santos, José Morales-Arilla and Zinedine Partipilo Cornielles

A full series listing is available at: www.cambridge.org/EEM

www.ingramcontent.com/pod-product-compliance
Ingram Content Group UK Ltd.
Pitfield, Milton Keynes, MK11 3LW, UK
UKHW022052020626
471784UK00009B/361
* 9 7 8 1 0 0 9 7 0 4 2 8 1 *